INTRODUCTORY

MICROECONOMICS

2 0 1 8 – 19

ii

Introductory Microeconomics
2018 – 19

Contents

Introduction

This book includes the lecture notes that I use and continually update. What you have in this book is exactly what I use in the lectures. At the back of the book are study aids that include example test questions and practice sets over the material.

Students may choose to use this outline in different ways. You may find it helpful to have it with you during the lectures. Or you may wish to use it to review after lectures, and/or in preparing for exams. My goal is to provide an overview of the lecture material, so that when you study you can have a concise exposition of what we covered. You should keep in mind that this is an *outline*, and sometimes key details explained during the class lectures do not appear in this book. Attending lectures and taking good notes are both critical for succeeding in the course.

As a companion to this outline, students are encouraged to get a standard Principles of Microeconomics textbook. Most textbooks are similar in their coverage, and there are few differences between various editions of textbooks. Older editions are much cheaper. Please ask for a recommendation.

This material was revised during the summer of 2018. Data on unemployment and taxes, and examples that we will discuss in the class, have been updated. There are a number of footnoted sources, and all URLs were working as of 7/26/18. Some policy issues, such as trade policy, are difficult to keep up-to-date, particularly with the volatility of the Trump administration.

My hope is that you find this to be a good alternative to a traditional textbook. Receipts from the book are used to support my other professorial duties, including research and academic conference expenses. I also contribute a portion to Omicron Delta Epsilon, the economics honor society at the College.

I am planning to expand this outline into a regular textbook. If you find any typos, or have any suggestions for improvements, please let me know. I hope you enjoy the class and this book!

Doug Walker
July 29, 2018

LECTURE A: OVERVIEW OF ECONOMIC ANALYSIS

The first section of the course is a general introduction to "the economic way of thinking." It is important to realize several things about economics from the outset. First, economics is a *social science*, and economic theory is the foundation for most business disciplines. Second, economics is more a method of analysis or thinking, than "job training" or the study of specific "topics" like the economy, the stock market, or money.

Economists study a variety of issues, including marriage and divorce, drug addiction, prostitution, environmental decay, political economy, and government policy. For example, your professor almost exclusively studies the economic and social impacts of legalized casino gambling. Almost any social phenomenon can be studied from an economics perspective.

Economics is the only social science for which a Nobel Prize is awarded. More important than any of the specific topics discussed, an understanding of economic theory helps you to develop critical thinking skills with which you may analyze a world of interesting topics.

The political and economic climate during the past decade has been interesting: slow recovery from the 2007-09 recession; health insurance overhaul; record budget deficits; the 2016 election; protectionist trade policies; and foreign policy changes, to name a few issues. Economic events can affect your life in serious and unexpected ways, and your generation will largely bear the consequences of current political decisions.

A good understanding of microeconomics will help you after college when you become a taxpayer and begin caring more about what politicians do. You will be better informed and able to analyze the likely economic impacts of government policies.

There is no obvious organization to this first lecture; the purpose here is to expose you to a number of different issues that help to form the foundation of economic theory.

The first thing you should learn in the course is that "economics" is all around you. Every decision that you make is an economic decision, whether or not it involves money.

- **The (Macro) Economy Today**

Before getting into the substance of the material for this course (microeconomics), it is worth taking some time to learn about what has been happening in U.S. macro-economy during the past few years. As you should be aware, the U.S. went through a serious recession that began in Dec. 2007, just before President Obama took office. The recession "officially" ended in June 2009. However, even five years after it ended, some key economic variables, such as unemployment, were still not back to pre-recession levels. It was a slow economic recovery.

The slow recovery worried many observers, especially since the policies enacted by the federal government seemed ineffective in helping the economy to grow. By 2018, however, things seemed more-or-less back to normal.

Recession is a technical term meaning negative economic growth (or negative gross domestic product [GDP] growth) for 6 months or longer. Usually, increasing unemployment and falling prices are characteristic of recessions.

The U.S. inflation-adjusted GDP growth rate since 2000 is shown in Figure A.1. The rate for the second quarter of 2018 (4.1%) is the highest it has been in several years. President Trump

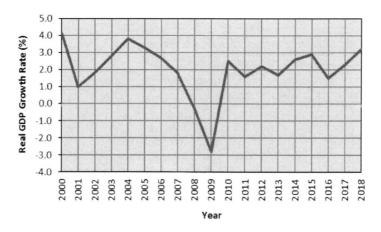

Figure A.1. U.S. real GDP growth rate, 2000-18
Data source: Bureau of Economic Analysis. The 2018 rate of 3.2% is the average of the first two quarters.

credits the tax cuts, regulatory cuts, and trade policies for the increased growth rate.

During the recession the U.S. unemployment rate peaked at 10.0% in October 2009. It has since fallen to 3.9%, as of June 2018. South Carolina's unemployment rate peaked at 11.7% in December 2009. By June 2018 it had fallen to 3.8%.

Figure A.2 shows the U.S. unemployment rate since 2000. Note that the unemployment rate was between 4% and 5% for several years shown in the graph. Economists consider 5% to be a "normal" rate of unemployment.

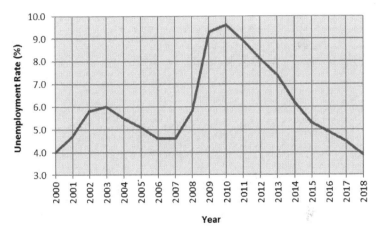

Figure A.2. U.S. unemployment rate, 2000-18
Data source: Bureau of Labor Statistics. The 2018 rate of 3.9% is for the second quarter.

Regardless of whether the economy is doing well or not, and whether democrats or republicans are running D.C., one thing remains constant: the federal government spends much more money than it brings in! As shown in Figure A.3, the federal budget deficit averaged $1.3 trillion from 2009-12. The 2018 federal budget includes $4.2t in spending (about $13,000 per resident) and $3.3t in taxes. Roughly $830 billion must be borrowed to fund spending in 2018. This represents about $2,500 of debt per resident.

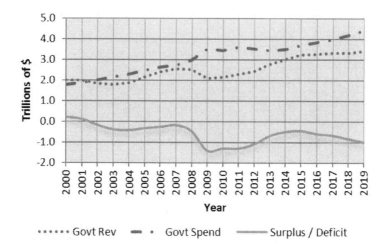

Figure A.3. U.S. federal fiscal trends, 2000-19
Data source: *2018 Economic Report of the President*, Table B-17; 2019 figures are government projections.

Large budget deficits are a real concern, because the money must eventually be repaid with higher future taxes. Before the Obama administration, Americans used to be concerned with $400 *billion* deficits. From 2002-08 the deficit was smaller, only close to $400b during two years. During the Clinton administration, from 1999 to 2001, we actually had a budget surplus! One thing is clear: both major political parties enjoy spending other people's money – and they rarely cut spending.[1]

When you add up annual *budget deficits*, the total is our *national debt*. As of summer 2018, our federal debt is over $21 TRILLION! That's $65,000 for each U.S. citizen.[2] Figure A.4 shows that, for the first time ever, our national debt surpassed GDP in 2013. (In Greece, this happened for the first time back in 1994; their 2016 debt:GDP ratio was over 1.8.)

---

[1] In 2009 Obama announced that he'd cut $100 million from the budget. For an interesting illustration that puts this amount of money in perspective, see https://www.youtube.com/watch?v=cWt8hTayupE.

[2] See http://www.usdebtclock.org for the current debt.

- Ex: a road map (or what you see on your GPS) is a model that is useful precisely because it ignores most aspects of reality – those which are irrelevant
- Ex: in modeling gambling behavior, we don't care about soft drink prices, new material used in bandages, etc.
- assumptions are starting points for developing models to test theories
    - two key assumptions used in all in economic models: rational behavior; *ceteris paribus*
    - rational behavior – acting in your self-interest
        - people compare expected costs and benefits (EC, EB) of a particular action, and act only if EB > EC; otherwise they're not rational
        - this doesn't rule out altruistic behavior, and it doesn't pertain only to monetary transactions
        - Ex: students coming to lecture (long-run benefits?)
        - Ex: giving money to a church/charity (self-interested, but not selfish)
    - *ceteris paribus* – "holding everything else constant"
        - you must isolate changes because the world is so complicated
        - with an understanding of the important individual determinants of behavior, we can better explain and predict behavior
        - Ex: considering the impact of introducing casinos on lottery sales, assume no change in people's incomes
- by using theories, models, and assumptions, economic analysis aims to explain and predict behavior
    - most interesting applications are policy changes

- **Examples of "Rationality Riddles"**
  - ○ You should assume people are rational and know what they're doing; don't just assume they're stupid
    - ■ Ex: why do stores practice 99¢ pricing? (and why do people do it for cars and real estate?)

Emerald Cut 11.85ct
IF Clarity, G Color Diamond
Platinum Solitaire Ring -
$819,999.99

Features: Only One Available,
IGI Value: $1,258,545

Figure A.5. Costco illustrates 99¢ pricing
Source: Costco.com, 2/19/16.

    - ■ Ex: Why have companies advertised that they have been corrupt, offer crappy products, or have otherwise done a bad job? (Buick[3], Domino's Pizza[4], Uber[5], Wells Fargo[6], Facebook[7])
      - ● …why would anyone use Wells Fargo still?
    - ■ Ex: Why do some bars put prices on menus for wine, but not beer?
    - ■ Ex: Why do some restaurants include tax in their prices (Warehouse), but others don't (Republic)?
      - ● see Figure A.6

---

[3] https://www.youtube.com/watch?v=q2nypLMEMr0

[4] https://www.youtube.com/watch?v=z3GcLH_834E

[5] https://www.youtube.com/watch?v=WMZyw5lPKgE

[6] https://www.youtube.com/watch?v=1rrivHxCeeY

[7] https://www.youtube.com/watch?v=Q4zd7X98eOs

```
        WE ARE WAREHOUSE
Join us on Sundays for Brunch 11am-4pm!

Server: Left Bar        12/14/2015
B4 Cp1/1                     9:08 PM
Guests: 1
                        #30070

El Conquistador              8.50
Employees CK                 8.50

Subtotal                    17.00
Tax                          0.00

Total                       17.00

Balance Due         17.00

            THANK YOU!
HAVE YOUR EVENT AT WAREHOUSE!
Email team@wearewarehouse.com
          (843) 202-0712
        wearewarehouse.com
          @team_warehouse
```

```
    Republic Garden & Lounge
         843-724-7400

Server: Catelen          08/25/2015
Cashier: Left Bar Out
Tbl 23/1                     6:14 PM
Guests: 1
                        #10006

Herradura Blanco             5.00
Gl. Champagne                6.50

Subtotal                    11.50
Tax                          1.46

Total                       12.96

Balance Due         12.96

     Thank you. Please return
   with this receipt in the next
   90 days and receive 20% off your
   next tab. Happy hour and bottle
     service not included.
```

Figure A.6. Receipts from Warehouse, which includes taxes in the prices, and Republic, which does not

- **Economic Analysis: The Basics (continued)**
  - There are two major branches of economics
    - micro and macro
  - Two types of statement
    - positive statements
      - can be tested and shown to be right or wrong
      - Ex: the unemployment rate is currently 5%
    - normative statements
      - are beliefs/opinions about what "should be" or what's "fair"
      - economists often disagree on what the proper role of government is
      - Ex: government should do more to lower unemployment
    - Ex: "the sales tax at restaurants is 11%" vs "the sales tax at restaurants is too high"
  - "Economic efficiency" is a major goal in economics
    - technological efficiency means producing the most possible given the inputs being used
    - allocative efficiency means we're producing what consumers want

- Adam Smith's "invisible hand" concept – that individuals' behavior when acting in their own self-interest is often consistent with the "public good"
  - this is a very important insight that you should gain through learning about how markets work – a primary goal of this class

- **Opportunity Cost**
  - This may be the most important idea in economics!
  - Defined as the highest valued-alternative use of resources foregone in making any choice
  - "Cost" in economics means full opportunity cost
    - "explicit costs" are like accounting costs ($)
    - "implicit costs" are the value of non-$ resources
    - Ex: Cru Café for dinner (parking, wait time, menu prices)
    - Ex: coming to the lecture
    - Ex: getting a college degree
      - is it rational to be in college if you don't expect to increase your salary?
    - Ex: why do salaries vary so much for professors of the same rank but of different disciplines?
      - CofC (2014) faculty salaries in different disciplines[8]: English, Teacher Ed, Philosophy, Anthropology ($60K); French ($52K); Accounting/Finance ($130K); Economics ($85K)
      - faculty salaries may reflect what graduates' relative salaries are likely to look like
    - Ex: the top 14 earning SC state employees get at least $400,000; 11 of these people are either coaches or athletic directors.

---

[8] Data source: http://www.admin.sc.gov/accountability-portal/state-salaries. College of Charleston is listed as "University of Charleston." USC's football coach Will Muschamp earns the top salary in 2018 (state-funded), $1.1 million.

"No one knows his place in society, his class position or social status, nor does anyone know his fortune in the distribution of natural assets and abilities, his intelligence, strength, and the like."

- the initial status quo is called the "original position"
- would you want some basic social safety net?
  - Ex: minimum amount of food or income provided, financed by taxes?
  - Ex: basic health insurance?
  - Ex: equal treatment under law?
- In "Why Does Johnny So Rarely Learn any Economics," Heyne argues that most people do not understand how an economy works, so they should not have input in making the rules affecting the economy
- Libertarians argue for a minimal role of government
  - enforce contracts
  - provide national defense
  - a basic "social safety net"
- Others argue for a much larger role of government
  - provide "free" health care
  - guarantee a "fair wages" for everyone
  - limit salaries of CEOs, etc.
- The U.S. Constitution outlined the rights of people and the limitations to government power
  - we've moved far away from the Constitution
  - consider "You're Afraid of Power, Not Trump"
- A solid understanding of economics is important for understanding how a just society could be organized

- **Forms of Government**[14,15]
  - ○ Although we will not go into much detail about various forms of government, it's worth defining a few
    - ▪ Authoritarian – state authority is imposed onto many aspects of citizens' lives
    - ▪ Communist – the state plans and controls the economy and a single – often authoritarian – party holds power; state controls are imposed with the elimination of private property and capital, while claiming to make progress toward a higher social order in which all goods are equally shared by the people (i.e., a classless society)
    - ▪ Democratic Republic – the supreme power rests in the body of citizens entitled to vote for officers and representatives responsible to them
    - ▪ Dictatorship – a ruler or small clique wield absolute power, not restricted by a constitution or laws
    - ▪ Fascism – characterized by dictatorial power, forcible suppression of opposition and control of industry and commerce.
    - ▪ Federal republic – the powers of the central government are restricted, and the component parts (states, colonies, or provinces) retain a degree of self-government; ultimate sovereign power rests with the voters who choose their government representatives
    - ▪ Marxism – Karl Marx viewed the struggle of workers as a progression of historical forces that would proceed from a class struggle of the

---

[14] This is a very short discussion of a very complex topic. These definitions are quoted or paraphrased from the CIA's *The World Factbook*, https://www. cia.gov/library/publications/the-world-factbook/docs/ notesanddefs.html, search for "government type". The definition here of "fascism" is from Wikipedia.

[15] John Stossel has a good short video on the "Deadly-isms" at http://reason. com/reasontv/2017/12/19/stossel-the-deadly-isms.

proletariat (workers) exploited by capitalists (business owners), to a socialist "dictatorship of the proletariat," to, finally, a classless society (Communism)

- Socialism – the means of planning, producing, and distributing goods is controlled by a central government that theoretically seeks a more just and equitable distribution of property and labor; in reality, most socialist governments have ended up being no more than dictatorships over workers by a ruling elite.

- Totalitarianism – government seeks to subordinate the individual to the state by controlling not only all political and economic matters, but also the attitudes, values, and beliefs of its population

24

APPENDIX TO LECTURE C
Deriving the Supply Curve from the Firm's Cost Curves

In this appendix we go into more detail in explaining why the supply curve has a positive slope and how firms make production decisions in an effort to maximize profit. This material is more concise than the typical textbook presentation; for more details, see a principles text's chapters on perfect competition.

- **Marginal Cost and Average Cost**
  - Consider production costs for the taco food truck, illustrated in Figure C.A1, which initially decrease as Q increases
    - there is some initial "learning," by cooks so MC tends to fall initially, up to 3 units
      - we use small Q, to keep the math simple
    - there may also be efficiencies from hiring additional workers (e.g., specialization)

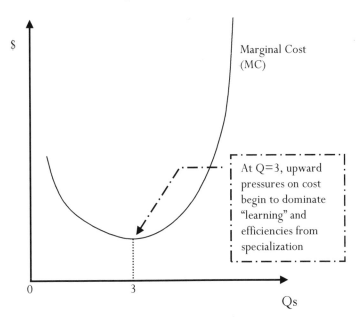

Figure C.A1. Marginal cost (MC) of production

- o Eventually, MC begins to increase, as some cost effects begin to dominate the learning and efficiencies
  - overcrowding (workers must wait to use the stove)
  - overtime or hiring workers for late shifts
  - the need to hire more talented/expensive workers
  - necessity to purchase more efficient capital
  - need for more managers or layers of management
- o Each factory (e.g., food truck) has some theoretical physical limit, in terms of quantity of production
  - at this point, the MC would become vertical
  - Ex: Consider growing a crop in a small area like a trash can; to increase Q, MC is going to rise
  - marginal product of labor ($MP_L = \Delta TP/\Delta L$) increases initially, then begins to fall off
- o Next consider what average cost (AC) would look like, given the shape of the MC curve
  - think about marginal GPA (current semester) and your average GPA (overall)
  - mathematically, $MC = \Delta TC/\Delta Q$ and $AC = TC/Q$
  - see the data in Table C.A1, which could represent a typical MC curve

Table C.A1. Production costs

Q	MC ($=\Delta TC/\Delta Q$)	TC ($=\Sigma MC$)	AC ($=TC/Q$)
1	$10	$10	$10.00
2	9	19	9.50
3	6	25	8.33
4	8	33	8.25
5	12	45	9.00

  - If you plot the data in Table C.A1, it would result in something like Figure C.A2

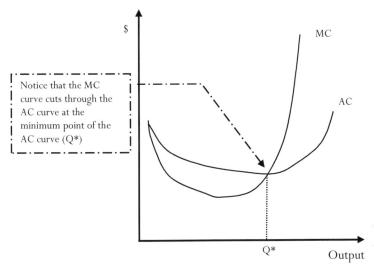

Figure C.A2. Marginal and average cost curves

- **Production Decisions and Profit Maximization**
  - Consider how a profit-maximizing firm decides whether or not to open for business
    - compare AC to P; understand that P=AR=MR
      - open if P ≥ min AC
  - If the firm can *potentially* make a profit, it can determine the profit-maximizing Q by comparing MC to P (again, keep in mind P=AR=MR)
    - profit maximization occurs where *P=MC*
  - "Break-even" example (Figure C.A3)
    - in economics this actually means the market average rate of return (say 5 or 6%), so firms are earning a "normal rate of profit"
    - in this situation, there is no incentive for the firm to leave the industry
    - there's also no incentive for new firms to enter this industry

44

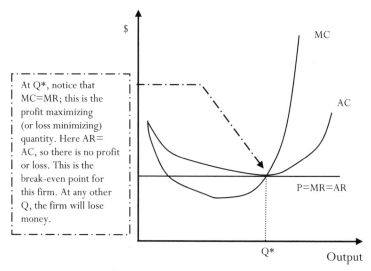

At Q*, notice that MC=MR; this is the profit maximizing (or loss minimizing) quantity. Here AR= AC, so there is no profit or loss. This is the break-even point for this firm. At any other Q, the firm will lose money.

Figure C.A3. A firm breaks even producing at Q*

- if the market price and firm's cost curves are as shown above, and the firm does not produce at Q* (where MR=MC), then it earns an economic loss, as shown below in Figure C.A4

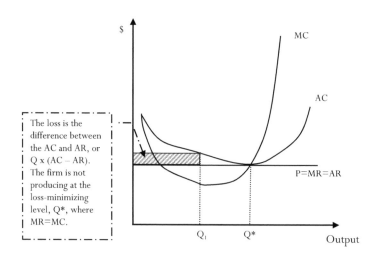

The loss is the difference between the AC and AR, or Q x (AC – AR). The firm is not producing at the loss-minimizing level, Q*, where MR=MC.

Figure C.A4. A firm suffers an economic loss producing at Q1

- In Figure C.A5 we shift the AC slightly higher and look again; even if the firm follows the profit-maximization rule (produce Q where MR=MC), it still earns a loss
  - the loss area would be larger at any other Q

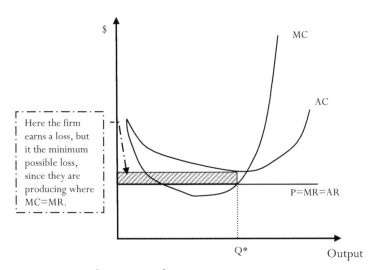

Figure C.A5. A firm earns a loss at Q*

- In some cases, it may be in the firm's best interest to remain open even if it is losing money
  - this would be true if the average variable cost (AVC) was lower than P, at Q*
    - AVC isn't shown in any of these figures, but the TC discussed earlier is composed of variable (labor) and fixed cost (capital) components
  - in this case, the firm can't cover its AC, but it can cover the variable portion, so producing loses less money than shutting down
  - Ex: suppose daily revenue is $100, variable costs are $40 per day, fixed costs are $80 per day
    - produce and lose $20; shut down and lose $80
- The firm shown in Figure C.A6 earns an "economic profit" in excess of the "normal rate of profit"

46

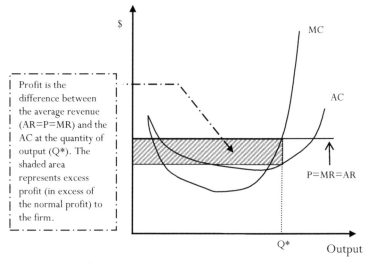

> Profit is the
> difference between
> the average revenue
> (AR=P=MR) and the
> AC at the quantity of
> output (Q*). The
> shaded area
> represents excess
> profit (in excess of
> the normal profit) to
> the firm.

Figure C.A6. A firm earning economic profit

- if existing firms in an industry are making a profit then new firms will be attracted to the industry

- **Deriving the Supply Curve**
  - o If the firm always produces at the profit-maximizing quantity (where MR=MC), whatever the market price, then it is easy to derive the S curve
  - o S *is* the MC curve above the minimum of the AC curve
    - recall that each firm produces up to the point at which P=MC in order to maximize profit
    - also recall that a supply curve indicates the maximum quantity a firm is willing to produce or sell at each P
  - o The dark-shaded MC curve in Figure C.A7 is the S curve

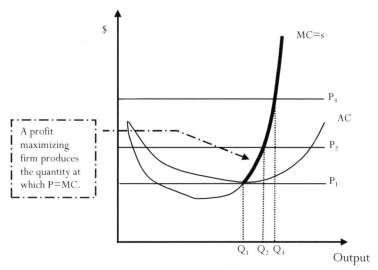

Figure C.A7. The supply curve is part of the MC curve

- **Firm Profit and Long-Run Equilibrium**
  - Summing all firms' individual supply curves (s) yields the market supply curve (S)
    - since economic profits will attract entry into the industry, $\Rightarrow \underset{\rightarrow}{S}$, and losses will cause exit from the industry so that $\underset{\leftarrow}{S}$, then in the absence of other supply changes or changes in demand, in the long-run, the market will look like the Figure C.A8
    - suppose 5 identical firms operate in the market, as pictured in the right panel of Figure C.A8
    - suppose the initial price is P_1; the firm would earn an economic profit
    - this attracts new firms to the industry, which increases S (rightward shift), pushing P down
    - new firms continue entering the industry until the price falls to where all firms in the industry are earning the normal rate of profit
    - the long-run equilibrium is shown in Figure C.A8, where Qe=25

48

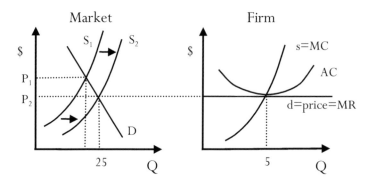

Figure C.A8. The industry and an individual firm in long-run equilibrium

- **Rates of Profit Across Industries**
  - As noted above, the normal rate of profit within an industry is maybe 5-6%
  - The rate is likely to be similar across industries
    - firms earning less profit will leave the industry
    - if firms in the industry are earning above the inter-industry average rate of profit, more firms will be attracted to the profitable industry
  - In a 2013 survey about profits, the public seemed to think the average company makes a 36% profit (!)[19]
    - data from this survey suggest that the average profit rate across 212 industries was 6.5%

- **Perfect Competition**
  - The market shown above is what economists call "perfect competition"
    - firms in competitive markets are "price takers"
      - they can sell as much as they want at the market price (Pe), but none at any price higher than Pe
    - the product is homogeneous

---

[19] https://www.aei.org/publication/the-public-thinks-the-average-company-makes-a-36-profit-margin-which-is-about-5x-too-high/

- since their products and prices are the same, firms do not advertise in competitive markets
- market entry and exit are free of barriers
  - This model of a perfectly competitive market is a benchmark for comparison
  - Ex: stock markets, commodity markets, gasoline?
    - but markets for other goods are usually not perfectly competitive

- **Monopoly**
  - This is the opposite extreme of perfect competition
    - a monopoly market has only one seller
    - to maximize profit, the monopolist chooses the Q where MR=MC, and charges the willingness to pay associated with that Q, found on the D curve
  - Compared to a perfectly competitive market, a monopolistic market will have higher prices and fewer transactions (less output), as in Figure C.A9

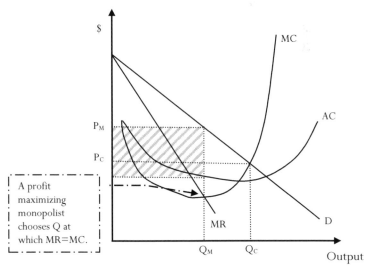

Figure C.A9. A monopolist's price, quantity, and profit, compared to a competitive market

- o We discuss monopolies later in the course under "market failures"

- **Input Costs and the Supply Curve, Revisited**
  - o Look back in Lecture C, "determinants of supply"
    - ▪ does this appendix help you understand why, when input prices rise, S of the good using the input falls?
      - • if not, study more!
  - o The supply curve is just a cost curve, and when $\underset{\leftarrow}{S}$, it means marginal costs are higher

LECTURE D: MARGINAL BENEFIT AND DEMAND

In this section, we develop the demand curve and explain its slope and causes for change. Just as with supply, understanding what causes changes in the demand curve is critical for understanding how markets work.

- **Demand**
  - o Demand is the maximum quantity an individual is *willing and able* to purchase at various prices
    - don't confuse "need" with "demand"
  - o The law of demand states that, *ceteris paribus*, <u>price</u> is negatively related to <u>quantity demanded</u>, for any good or service
    - so a price increase causes quantity demanded to fall:
      $$P{\uparrow} \Rightarrow Qd \seardown$$
    - vice versa, $P{\downarrow} \Rightarrow Qd \searrow$
    - a D curve can be drawn to show the law of demand (the relationship between P and Qd)
  - o Suppose Figure D.1 illustrates your demand for tacos
    - aside from the fact that it reflects the law of demand, why intuitively would you expect a demand curve to have a negative slope?
    - what happens to marginal benefit (the benefit of each additional unit) of consumption as $Q \atop \rightarrow$?
      - law of decreasing marginal benefit (MB)

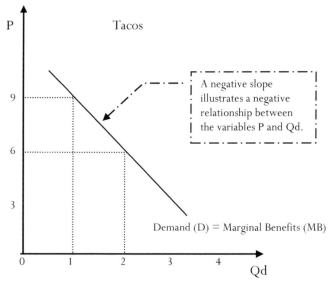

Figure D.1. Demand curve (D) or marginal benefits (MB) curve

- o Ex: If you're stranded in the desert without water
    - how much benefit would the first glass give?
    - what about the second, third, and additional glasses of water?
    - if you graph this "marginal benefits" curve, what happens as $\underset{\rightarrow}{Q}$?
    - based on this, what would happen to a person's willingness to pay for these different glasses of water?

- **Determinants of Demand**
    - o A <u>change in quantity demanded</u> (ΔQd) refers to a <u>movement along the demand curve</u>, caused <u>only</u> by a change in price (ΔP)
        - P↑ ⇒ $\underset{\nwarrow}{Qd}$; so then if P↓ ⇒ $\underset{\searrow}{Qd}$
        - see Figure D.2

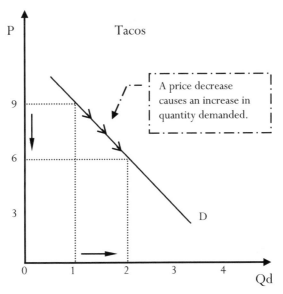

Figure D.2. Increase in quantity demanded (Qd) due to a decrease in price

- o   Any change other than price that affects demand causes a <u>change in demand</u> (ΔD – a <u>shift of the demand curve</u>)
    - ▪   an increase in demand, $\underset{\rightarrow}{D}$, is a right shift
        - •   see Figure D.3
        - •   at a particular P (holding P constant), now buyers are willing to purchase a greater Q
        - •   or to be willing to purchase a particular Q (holding Q constant), now consumers are willing to pay a higher P
    - ▪   a decrease in demand, $\underset{\leftarrow}{D}$, is a left shift

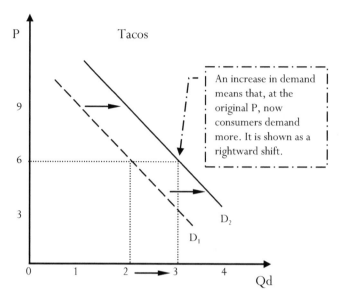

Figure D.3. An increase in demand, due to a change in a non-price determinant

- o There are five "shift factors" for the demand curve:
  - ▪ Δ in the number of consumers
    - • if it rises, so will D; vice versa
  - ▪ Δ in tastes and preferences
    - • Ex: fads, medical evidence, etc.
  - ▪ ΔP expectations
    - • if you expect in the future P will ↑, current $\frac{D}{\rightarrow}$
    - • Ex: if you expect gas prices to be higher next week, you'll fill up your tank now (current demand will increase)
  - ▪ Δ in consumer income
    - • "normal goods" are those for which $\frac{D}{\rightarrow}$ when income ↑
      - o Ex: latest iPhone; meals at FIG in Charleston, Chinaco tequila; new video games

- "inferior goods" are those for which $\underset{\leftarrow}{D}$ when income ↑
  - Ex: Spam; Yugo cars; lunches at a college cafeteria; generic brand foods
- ΔP of related goods; for two goods, A & B...
  - when P_A↑ and $\underset{\rightarrow}{D_B}$, A and B are substitutes
    - Ex: Coke & Pepsi; gasoline & air travel
  - when P_A↓ and $\underset{\rightarrow}{D_B}$, A and B are complements
    - Ex: camera & film; textbooks and tuition; DVDs & DVD players; gasoline & SUVs
- We can go from an "individual" demand curve to a "market" demand curve by summing horizontally the individual demand curves
  - at each P, we want to add the Qd of all individuals in the market; the result is the market D curve

- **Demand vs Quantity Demanded**
  - "Demand" or D refers to the *entire curve*
  - "Quantity demanded" or Qd refers to a *point on the curve*

- **Consistency is Important in Using Graphs**
  - Always label all axes and curves!
  - Think of an increase in D or S as a <u>rightward shift of the curve</u>; a decrease is a <u>leftward shift</u>
  - An increase in Qd or Qs is <u>rightward movement along the curve</u>; a decrease is <u>leftward movement along the curve</u>

LECTURE E: MARKETS AND PRICE DETERMINATION

In this lecture we put together supply and demand curves, to see how markets work and how prices are determined. This section assumes you have a thorough understanding of the previous two. Much of the remainder of the course relies on an understanding of this section.

- **Market Equilibrium**
  - Putting S and D on the same graph illustrates a "market"
    - the intersection of S & D is called <u>equilibrium</u>
    - the equilibrium price (Pe) is the price at which Qd=Qs; this is called the equilibrium quantity (Qe)
    - see Figure E.1
  - If P>Pe, then there is a <u>surplus</u> in the market (Qs>Qd)
  - If P<Pe, then there is a <u>shortage</u> in the market (Qs<Qd)

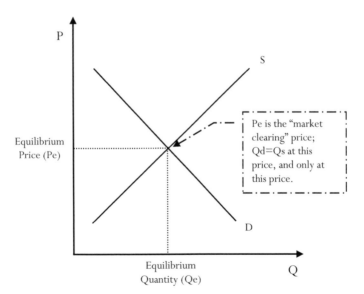

Figure E.1. Market equilibrium

- **Mutually Beneficial, Voluntary Transactions**
  - These are "good" for society
    - the more of these, the better; when this number is maximized, we have efficiency – the best possible outcome for that market
  - Market transactions are the result of self-interest
    - consumers want to maximize their utility or benefits from consumption (and a limited budget)
    - sellers want to maximize their profits
      - Adam Smith's famous passage:

        "It is not from the benevolence of the butcher, the brewer, or the baker, that we expect our dinner, but from their regard to their own interest"[20]

  - How many mutually beneficial voluntary transactions occur at each price?
  - At P>Pe, which side of the market is "unsatisfied" (i.e., can't find someone else to transact with)
  - Who's "unsatisfied" when P<Pe?
  - We discuss the benefits from market transactions in more detail in Lecture F

- **How Changes in S or D Affect Equilibrium P & Q**
  - Changes in D or S will cause the Pe and Qe to change
    - when $D_{\rightarrow}$, Pe↑ and $Qe_{\rightarrow}$; when $D_{\leftarrow}$, Pe↓ and $Qe_{\leftarrow}$
    - see Figure E.2: when $S_{\rightarrow}$, Pe↓ and $Qe_{\rightarrow}$
    - when $S_{\leftarrow}$, then Pe↑ and $Qe_{\leftarrow}$
  - Like a thermometer reflects temperature, prices reflect the reflect relative scarcity of goods and services
    - a high price does not "cause" scarcity, it is a reflection of scarcity

---

[20] *An Inquiry into the Nature and Causes of the Wealth of Nations* (1776, book I, ch. II)

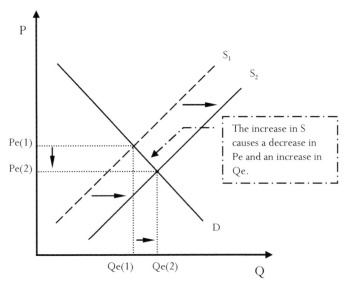

Figure E.2. An increase in supply (S) causes a decrease in Pe and an increase in Qe

- o Aside from finding the new P & Q, you must understand *how* P & Q adjust
  - ▪ this applies, generally, when P ≠ Pe (when there is either a surplus or shortage)
- o Consider Figure E.3, which illustrates a $\underset{\rightarrow}{D}$ for cars
  - ▪ once $\underset{\rightarrow}{D}$, Pe(1) is no longer an equilibrium; there is an immediate shortage in the market
  - ▪ both suppliers and consumers will respond
    - • consumers, noticing they can't find the car at any of the dealers, will start offering more money to get the car, or to be put at the top of the waiting list; they might even start offering sticker price or higher
    - • sellers, who notice that they cannot keep the car in stock at the original price, and that consumers are coming in and offering higher prices, will of course raise their prices

60

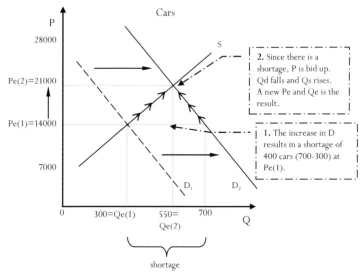

Figure E.3. An increase in demand causes an immediate shortage at Pe(1), causing a price adjustment

- the price is bid-up by consumers and producers, and P↑, as Qs↗ while Qd↖
- eventually, the shortage is eliminated as the price adjusts

o What would happen to P & Q if S rises in the market?

- at the original price, the S increase would create a surplus
- now with excess supplies, the dealers slash prices, and put things "on sale"
- consumers see advertising, know they can get a good deal, and bid price down
- as P↓, Qs↙ and Qd↘; eventually the surplus disappears

- **Changes in S & D Simultaneously**
    o The analysis becomes more difficult
    - you can only determine the direction of change in one variable (either Pe or Qe), not both

- the direction of change in these variables depends on the relative magnitude of the curve shifts
- it's easy to analyze if you remember the individual effects of ΔS and ΔD on Pe and Qe
- so if $\underset{\rightarrow}{D}$ and $\underset{\rightarrow}{S}$ simultaneously, then you know $\underset{\rightarrow}{Qe}$, but the ΔPe is indeterminate
  - if $\underset{\rightarrow}{D}$ more than $\underset{\rightarrow}{S}$, then P↑ since the demand effect would dominate the supply effect on P

- **"Perfect Competition" and the Market Model**
  ○ We're making a few assumptions; refer back to the Appendix to Lecture C…
    - "many" consumers and producers → no individual control over P
    - homogeneous goods and services
    - consumers and producers are "informed"
  ○ These obviously don't apply to most markets; some are closer than others to perfect competition
  ○ This is a "benchmark" which we use to judge the efficiency of market outcomes.

LECTURE F: MARKETS AND ECONOMIC EFFICIENCY

This is the most important section in the course. It is critical that you attend all sessions for this lecture. Now we put together all of the previous topics to develop a more in-depth understanding of why markets are "efficient," and why the individual participants benefit from market transactions.

Once you've studied the material for this lecture, you should be able to discuss this sensibly: *"What is the function of prices and profits in allocating scarce resources to suppliers and consumers in a market economy?"* Everything in the course until now has been leading up to this issue. If you understand this, you probably understand more about economics than 95% of the U.S. population.

- **The Functions of Prices and Profits**
  - o Prices represent <u>information to producers</u> trying to decide what, how much, and how to produce
    - ▪ prices and profits signal to suppliers which goods & services are valued by consumers
      - • profit is the key incentive for producers
    - ▪ prices are instrumental in determining the quantity produced
      - • to maximize profits, each firm produces up to where P=MC, as shown in the Appendix to Lecture C
      - • this issue is discussed in the "Springfield farming lecture" (below)
    - ▪ the "how to produce" deals with using K and L; we won't discuss this decision much
  - o Prices provide important <u>information to consumers</u>, too
    - ▪ they signals the relative scarcity of goods & services
    - ▪ prices allocate goods & services only to the consumers with the most intense demand for the products
  - o Prices serve a critical <u>allocative function</u> in markets, determining who will produce and consume

- input resources are allocated only to low-cost firms who can make a profit at the market price
  - if a firm earns losses, it won't be able to pay for inputs into the long-run
- goods & services to the people with the greatest expected benefit and willingness & ability to pay
- the result is "allocative efficiency"

- **Consumer Surplus and Producer Surplus**
  - In Lecture E we briefly discussed mutually beneficial voluntary transactions
    - we now look into more detail how market participants benefit
  - CS and PS are critical concepts of "welfare economics" that we will use for policy analysis later in the course
    - Note that these "surpluses" have nothing to do with $Qs>Qd$; this is a completely different concept
  - Consumer surplus (CS) is the difference between the maximum consumers are <u>willing to pay</u> (indicated on the D curve), and what they <u>actually pay</u> (P)
    - think about it if you were unaware what the price is, and you decide you want a taco; how much would you be willing to pay?
      - then you find the food truck and see the P
    - CS is the area under the D curve above the price line (see Figure F.1)
    - CS is a benefit to consumers, consistent with common sense: consumers like lower prices

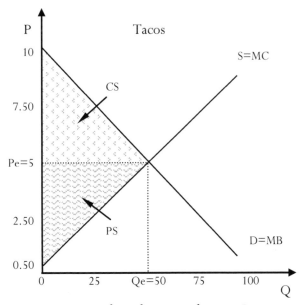

Figure F.1. Consumer and producer surpluses at Pe

- CS is "in your face" at some retailers
  - Ex: Ross, Big Lots, Marshall's, Burlington: price tags "compare at $12; our price $8"
    - $4 CS in this example, if you value it at $12
    - value is subjective; you may value it at $0
  - Ex: Figure F.2 shows a Ross tag (with a typo?)

Figure F.2. A price tag from Ross as an illustration of CS

66

- Producer surplus (PS) is the difference between what sellers <u>actually receive</u> (indicated by P) and the <u>minimum they would be willing to accept</u> (MC curve)
  - PS is the area above the S curve below the P line
  - PS is a benefit to producers – it's profit; consistent with the idea that sellers like higher prices
- Calculating CS and PS values in Figure F.1
  - area of a triangle $= \frac{1}{2}$ (base)(height)
    - CS $= \frac{1}{2}$ (50)(5) $= \$125$, assuming D intersects the P axis at $10
    - PS $= \frac{1}{2}$ (50)(4.50) $= \$112.50$, assuming S intersects the P axis at $0.50
- Using CS and PS
  - PS and CS are measures of the welfare of those groups, so the "total surplus" (PS + CS) is a measure of total social welfare
    - the larger the total surplus, the better
    - at any P≠Pe, the total surplus <u>must</u> be lower than at Pe
  - one reason people may think "profit" is taking advantage of people is that PS is clearly visible
    - firms have to report profits and pay taxes; consumers don't have to report CS to the IRS
    - CS is perhaps less tangible, but no less real

- **"Springfield Farming Lecture"**
  - Here we examine some individual farmers' production decisions to see how government production decisions would differ from market decisions
    - This lecture is extremely important, so I've written it out…
    - It's based on a brief discussion from Landsburg's *The Armchair Economist*, pp. 93-94

Springfield Farming: Efficiency in Production and Consumption

We wish to consider a simple economy with two farmers. Whether government or the individual farmers make the production decisions can have an enormous impact on the outcome for this market. By extension, this example will help you understand the relative likely performance of market-oriented versus government-run economies. A fundamental point to this analysis is that prices serve a critical function in well-functioning markets.

1 "Socialist" economy

First consider a socialist world, in which there is no private property ownership, and no markets. A czar (dictator) will determine who produces and consumes and in what quantities. For simplicity, let's assume that wheat is the only good produced and consumed in our economy. (Although we only consider one good, the analysis would apply to all goods produced.) Looking at production only, say that Willie and Flanders are the only two wheat producers. Remember that since there is no private property, we assume the farmers simply produce the quantities they're assigned, and they are paid based on the costs they incur or the time they spend.

If you were the "wheat czar" in charge of assigning the production quantities for the farmers, how would you go about it? Suppose that you are a benevolent dictator and your goal as wheat czar is to *minimize total cost of aggregate wheat production*. You are concerned with economic (productive) efficiency. That is, you want to produce a given amount of wheat for the minimum possible total cost (*TC*). Suppose your superior tells you that you are responsible for producing 6 bushels of wheat this year. Given this goal, how would you assign wheat production to the two farmers? (Notice that we must *assume* some quantity of wheat to produce. How would we know the correct amount?)

In order to obtain your goal of efficiency, you must look at the *marginal production costs* for the two farmers. Recall the marginal cost (*MC*) curve and the characteristics of its up-sloping section (i.e., $MC \uparrow$ as $Q \uparrow$, since as producers increase quantity, they must bid away more resources from alternative uses, pushing prices up). Now, given the information in the Table F.1, we can see how to make the production decision.

Recall that your goal is to minimize the total cost of producing 6 bushels of wheat, whoever produces them. Suppose you tell Willie to produce all of it; *TC* of production in this case is $25. This would certainly be better than having Flanders produce all the wheat—it would cost him $33. But remember that we're not focusing on the costs to particular farmers. Rather, we care only about the total society wide cost of producing the wheat.

So let's say you initially decide to have Willie produce all the wheat. Notice that the *MC* to him of that last bushel is $7. If you were to have Flanders produce one bushel (his first), it would cost him only $2. So why not have Willie produce only 5 bushels and let Flanders produce 1 for the total of 6 bushels. This will save society $5: we decrease our cost by $7 by having Willie *not* produce his 6th bushel, but we add a cost of $2 since Flanders will now be producing his first bushel. The *TC* is now only $20 ($18 *TC* for Willie, and $2 *TC* for Flanders), instead of $25, when Willie was producing all the wheat. We can do the same thing again – continue substituting Flanders' (cheap) wheat for Willie's (expensive) wheat. When do we stop substituting?

Table F.1. Production costs for wheat in Springfield

Bushel	Willie		Flanders	
#	MC	TC	MC	TC
1	$1	$1	$2	$2
2*	$2	$3	$3	$5
3	$4	$7	$4	$9
4	$5	$12	$6	$15
5	$6	$18	$8	$23
6	$7	$25	$10	$33
7	$8	$33	$12	$45

* For example, to produce the second bushel, Willie must incur a $2 *MC*. This means that his total cost (*TC*) increases by $2; since the *MC* of the first unit was $1, his *TC* for producing two bushels is $3.

It turns out (you should make sure you understand how) the total production cost of 6 bushels of wheat is minimized – recall that this is our goal – when the MC of production for the two farmers is the same. Therefore, we want to assign a production level for which the MC of all producers is the same. Think about why this makes sense. What happens when we continue the substitution beyond this point? Suppose we are having Willie and Flanders produce 3 bushels each and then we decide to have Willie produce only 2 and have Flanders produce 4 bushels. How does this change our total production cost? We save $4 by having Willie *not* produce the 3rd bushel, but we increase our cost by $6 since Flanders will now be producing a 4th bushel – our total cost *increases* by $2. You should convince yourself that the best production allocation, from "society's" perspective, i.e., minimum total production cost, is to have each farmer produce 3 bushels of wheat. (Understand that the fact that both farmers are producing the same quantity [3] is purely coincidental; the equal MC is what is important for minimizing TC.) At any other combination of quantities, TC will be higher than the $16 at 3-3.

How likely are you (the wheat czar) to pick the correct quantity of production or the levels for each farmer? How would you know the farmers' MC curves? This would be impossible, especially in an economy where there are millions of goods and producers. Aside from quantities of production, how would you decide *which* goods to produce? Resources are limited. What we have is an "information problem," a result of *the absence of markets (and therefore price and profit signals)*, which makes it impossible for a socialist economy to work.

Suppose you go ahead and assign production levels for the wheat farmers. Then, after the wheat is harvested, you have to decide who gets to consume the wheat. How would you do this? Again, we don't have markets or prices. But in theory, you'd like to give the first bushel to the person that has the highest marginal utility (MU) of wheat, the next bushel would go to the person with the next highest MU_{wheat}, and so on, until everyone's MU_{wheat} is equal (recall that $MU \downarrow$ as $Q \uparrow$). But how could you possibly know everyone's MU_{wheat} – and for every other good? Efficiency in consumption, i.e., having the goods go to the people who value them the most, is very difficult without some mechanism other than a guess by the dictator. It would be good if we could have people express the levels of their desires.

So far we've illustrated how a socialist economy would ideally function: we'd have the lowest-cost producers producing our goods, and we'd have the goods going to the people who most desire them. We've also identified a few of the reasons why this is impossible to do with government direction.

2 Market economy

Now we'll consider a market economy (without czars directing production or consumption) with freely moving prices. In such an economy, we have millions of individual decision-makers. There are (assume) no government officials telling the citizens what or how much they should produce or consume. People produce things based on the expected profit (price minus cost of production), and buy things based on their desires and ability to pay. In our first example, we assumed a czar told the farmers how much to produce. Without someone telling the farmers they need to grow 6 bushels, won't there be a wheat shortage (or surplus)? How will they know how much to produce?

The answer to this question is the reason why a free market economy is the most successful economic framework in history. If we have prices, which are determined, as you know, by the interaction of supply and demand, efficient production of wheat – and every other product – is assured. How? Consider our wheat farmers Willie and Flanders. Suppose they have the same MCs as in the socialist economy we considered earlier. Do we want them to produce 6 bushels of wheat, like we were told to in the socialist economy? We don't know. No person could ever know how much wheat we *should* produce. Only the market can determine this. The interaction of self-interested individuals determines the "correct" amount of wheat production.

Suppose that as a result of the interaction between suppliers and consumers, the current market price of wheat is $6 per bushel. How much wheat will be produced in the market? To answer this, we must understand the incentives in a market economy. People are assumed to only have a concern for their own well-being. In the case of the farmers (and the producers of all goods), they want to maximize their profits. They could care less about "social efficiency" (minimizing total cost of aggregate production), which *was our only goal as czar*. How, then, would individual farmers decide how much to produce? Given the market price of $6, and using our previous production table, consider Table F.2.

How much wheat will each farmer produce? We'll look at Willie. (Similar logic would apply to Flanders and every other farmer and producer in every market of the economy.) First notice that, for each bushel of wheat grown, the farmer can sell it for $6. Willie is trying to maximize his profit. He must decide how much wheat to produce. Willie decides whether or not to produce the first bushel of wheat by comparing the price he can receive (his benefit) to the *MC* (his cost). Since he is rational, he will produce that first bushel only if *MB>MC*. The price (or marginal benefit) is $6, and his *MC* is $1, so profit is $5. So he plants the first bushel. Should he plant another? He'll receive $6

Table F.2. Market price and production costs for wheat

Bushel #	Price / Bushel*	Willie			Flanders		
		MC	TC	Unit Profit	MC	TC	Unit Profit
1	$6	$1	$1	$5	$2	$2	$4
2	$6	$2	$3	$4	$3	$5	$3
3	$6	$4	$7	$2	$4	$9	$2
4	$6	$5	$12	$1	$6	$15	$0
5	$6	$6	$18	$0	$8	$23	-$2
6	$6	$7	$25	-$1	$10	$33	-$4
7	$6	$8	$33	-$2	$12	$45	-$6

* We assume that the wheat market is large enough so that neither Willie nor Flanders can affect the market price of wheat. This is certainly a realistic assumption for many markets. Unit profit is the bushel price minus the marginal cost.

for that bushel, too, and it will cost him $2 to produce. For the second bushel, Willie will earn $4 profit ($6-2). It is then rational for him to plant the second bushel. He would keep making the production decision in this manner – comparing marginal benefit with marginal cost. *TC* is <u>not</u> relevant for his marginal production decision. How many bushels, then, will Willie plant? He would plant up until *P=MC*. From the table above, Willie should plant 5 bushels – just up to where *P=MC*. He would not, however, plant a 6th bushel, since it would decrease his profits. If he plants 5 bushels, his total profit is $12 ($5+4+2+1+0). If he continues planting, say up to 6 bushels, he'll earn a negative profit on the 6th bushel – his total profit there would be $11, less than when he produced only 5 bushels. All wheat farmers will go through a similar decision process. And each will produce up to where *P=MC*. If there is only one market price (and we're assuming there is), what conclusions can you make?

Willie will produce 5 bushels and Flanders will produce 4 to maximize profits. Recall that all farmers are concerned only with their individual profits. When we went through the production decisions above, there was no mention of social cost or total cost of production. At the market price of $6, 9 bushels are produced. But look: if we produce 9 bushels, when Willie produces 5 and Flanders produces 4, that *is* the minimum total (social) cost of producing 9 bushels! The *MC* for all farmers is equal. The greedy farmers have actually achieved social efficiency – the czar's goal – without even thinking about it and without any government intervention! Their only goal is to maximize profit, which they do by producing up to where *P=MC*. The only information they need is their own costs – which they are sure to know better than some czar. This illustration shows that the existence of prices and profits leads us to a socially efficient (cost minimizing) production solution.

A key point worth emphasizing here is that the price in the market was a key signal for the farmers to decide how much to produce. When government tries to make these decisions without the help of the price signal, they will get potentially disastrous results. Historically, countries whose governments tried to make all production decisions have not fared well. [21]

---

[21] A classic essay on the importance of price signals is Ludwig von Mises' "Economic Calculation in the Socialist Commonwealth" (1920).

As for consumers, consider an alternative to a czar deciding who gets what. Instead, if we have a market and a price of $6, then only those who are willing and able to pay $6 (or more) will receive any wheat (say bread). We expect consumers to buy wheat until their MU_{bread} (in dollar terms) becomes equal to the market price of bread. Given we would expect that the MU_{bread} will decrease as consumption increases, the result on the demand side will be analogous to the production side. Individuals will buy additional bread as long as the MU_{bread} is greater than or equal to the price. Then the MU_{bread} of all consumers will be equal, and equal to the price of bread. This result represents efficiency in the consumption of wheat/bread.

3 Markets, prices, and profits

Only the most efficient producers survive in a market economy. And only those consumers who are willing and able to pay a particular price will receive the product. This ensures that those who have the most intense desires will get the goods. Is it fair that some people have the desire but not the ability to pay? Consider how people obtain the "ability to pay". People who provide valuable goods or services to the market earn income with which they can buy goods and services. For example, brain surgeons provide a service that not many people can, and they are paid well for their skills. Bill Gates had a very important role in the development of the computer industry; he has been rewarded. But people who try to sell 486 computers would not be expected to do well in today's world. If a person is able to make a profit – by selling something that is valued by society – then that person gains increased purchasing power.

Bringing all of this together in a standard market diagram, we can illustrate how input resources and final goods and services are allocated. The most efficient producers are those who are willing to supply the good at the lowest price. Since producers maximize profit, then at a given market price, only those with relatively lower costs will be willing to supply. These suppliers are represented on the left part of the supply curve below Pe. The consumers who have the most desire and ability to pay are represented on the left part of the demand curve, above *Pe*. Anytime our market is not in equilibrium (at *Pe* and *Qe*), the actual quantity traded is less than it would be at *Pe*. This point is illustrated in Figure F.3, below.

- **Economic Efficiency: Transactions Approach**
  o The people who engage in transactions in the market are represented by:
    - the low MC producers (lower left-hand side of S)
    - the high MB consumers (upper left-hand side of D)
    - see Figure F.3

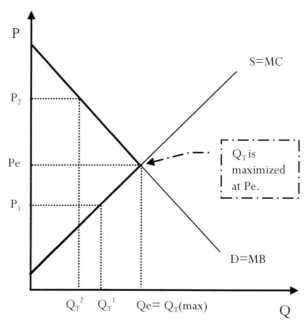

Figure F.3. The quantity of transactions (Q_T) at various prices

  o There are <u>no unsatisfied people in the market at Pe</u>
    - i.e., there isn't anyone in the market who wants to trade but can't find a partner
    - quantity of transactions (Q_T) is maximized at Pe

- all sellers willing to sell at Pe can sell all they want
- all buyers willing to pay Pe can buy all they want
  - this doesn't necessarily guarantee an "equitable" allocation of resources, but it is "efficient"
  - o Make certain you understand why the *number of mutually beneficial, voluntary transactions* is maximized at Pe
    - this relates to government laws that affect prices, which we discuss in a later lecture

- **Economic Efficiency: Cost-Benefit Approach**
  - o Recall that MB=D and MC=S; we can see economic efficiency from a "societal perspective"
  - o See Figure F.4
    - for the 4th unit, the MB of consumption > MC of production, so we should increase production & consumption – it produces a net benefit

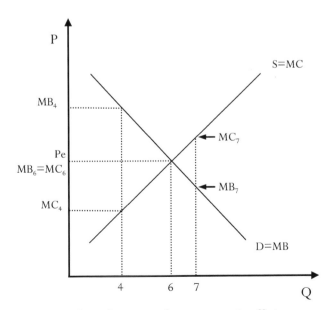

Figure F.4. Cost-benefit approach to economic efficiency

- for the 7th unit, however, MC>MB, so it's not in society's interest
- The socially optimal level of production/ consumption is where MC=MB, always at Pe
- MB of consumption = MC of production for 6th the unit

- **Net Surplus from Market Transactions**
  - Related to the costs and benefits of production and consumption from above, it is useful to consider the *total benefits and costs* from market transactions
  - See Figure F.5, which shows the taco market again
    - total benefit from consuming the 50 tacos is area A+B+C
      - total area under D, up to Qe
      - ($5 x 50) + ½ ($5)(50) = $375

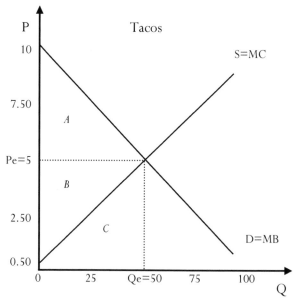

Figure F.5. Net benefit to society of the taco market

- total cost of producing the 50 tacos is area C
  - area under S, up to Qe
  - ($5 x 50) – ½ ($4.50)(50) = $137.50
- net benefit to society from the taco market is area A+B
  - $237.50 (calculated $375 - $137.50)
  - this is split between consumers (CS = area A) and producers (PS = area B)

- **Foundations of a Market Economy**
  - Freedom of choice is important so that individuals can pursue their own interests
    - the market produces what people want
    - in contrast, consider a "socialist" system where government makes production and consumption decisions without the aid of price signals
  - Private property rights (and enforcement) are important so that producers know their investment will be theirs tomorrow
    - who would want to build a factory in a country whose government could nationalize it?
  - Competition is an extremely important component of market economies
    - it forces producers to make better products
    - you must satisfy consumers to do well
      - consider which doctors serve you better: those where insurance pays it (regular doctor, hospitals), or those where insurance doesn't cover (plastic surgery or vision correction)
    - how about private versus public schools
      - why do teachers' unions oppose competition?
  - Entrepreneurship is taking risks to open a business, or the creativity to try something different
    - risky
    - taxes penalize success and reduce incentives

Figure F.6. Two very specialized stores in Charleston, selling honey and jerky; who would've guessed they'd survive?

- you take 100% of your losses, but only keep 60% of your gains (if taxes are 40%)
  - ○ Profits are the key incentive for producers
    - ▪ profitable firms tend to satisfy consumers' desires
    - ▪ profitable industries attract new firms
    - ▪ unprofitable firms close down, to the benefit of society
      - this frees up scarce resources for higher-valued uses
      - Ex: horse-drawn carriage industry
    - ▪ why do politicians sometimes vilify "profit" (e.g., banking, oil companies), while also having sympathy for failing companies (e.g., auto industry)?

- **Hazlitt, "How the Price System Works" (Ch. 15) and "The Function of Profits" (Ch. 22)**
  - ○ In the chapter, "How the Price System Works," Hazlitt discusses Robinson Crusoe's world
    - ▪ individuals & societies must allocate scarce resources; they face trade-offs
    - ▪ we are best served by specialization and trade
  - ○ In the long run, if productive resources are free to move among industries, we should expect about the same rate of profit in all industries – why?

- o The market and "invisible hand" tend to reward those who produce things valuable to society
  - "to those who do not, the invisible hand shows them its middle finger" (Todd Buchholz)
- o Profits represent incentives to produce; if you limit profits, then you limit the incentive to produce things that people want
- o From Hazlitt's chapter, The Function of Profits:

  "One function of profits, in brief, is to guide and channel the factors of production as to apportion the relative output of thousands of different commodities in accordance with demand. No bureaucrat, no matter how brilliant, can solve this problem arbitrarily. Free prices and free profits will maximize production and relieve shortages quicker than any other system. Arbitrarily fixed prices and arbitrarily limited profits can only prolong shortages and reduce production and employment."

- o Profits do not result only from higher prices; the introduction of efficiencies in production are a key to increasing profits (i.e., doing it better or more cheaply)

- **What About Equity?**
  - o We've talked a lot about efficiency, and markets are good at bringing about efficient outcomes
  - o What about equity? If you don't have any money, you don't "demand" anything
    - D is willingness *and ability* to pay
    - shouldn't we be more concerned with people who can't afford everything?
  - o Everyone makes choices and must prioritize
    - someone with a low income will probably not want $50 dinners at FIG; he has higher priorities
      - if given a gift certificate for FIG, he'd probably prefer to have cash to pay for something else

- o Concern for the poor is commendable
  - but blaming markets is misguided
  - wealth transfers can help most directly and efficiently
    - taxes
    - charities
- o Government policies often fail to meet their goals
  - Ex: inefficiencies, unintended consequences, corruption

- **Flaws in Consumers and Voters**
  - o Certainly, markets do not function perfectly, but they do work pretty well
    - what's the alternative?
  - o Mike Munger makes a compelling argument that "every flaw in consumers is worse in voters"[22]
    - consumers have limited information about the products they purchase
      - but they learn from mistakes
    - voters know almost nothing about how their candidates will act
  - o Examples Munger discusses:
    - asymmetric information
    - monopoly
    - seductive and misleading advertising
    - free stuff
  - o This suggests we should have at least as much faith in consumers and markets as we do in politicians and government

---

[22] http://www.learnliberty.org/blog/every-flaw-in-consumers-is-worse-in-voters/

LECTURE G: GOVERNMENT PRICE CONTROLS

In this section, we analyze government policies that affect prices directly. Given we have already discussed the efficient results from markets, you might be surprised that price controls are ever enacted. In this section, the distinction between politics and economics should become apparent.

Since this is one of our first looks into political issues, I should stress that what is important here is not the particular conclusions we find. What is important is that you understand how to perform economic analysis of government policy actions. Generally, our economic analysis will suggest that government usually does not choose very effective means to achieve its goals.

In most cases, price controls are enacted to transfer wealth to a particular group of people at the expense of everyone else. We'll show why popular government price controls are usually a very inefficient way to achieve their goal. Being a good economist means looking for better alternative ways to achieve a goal – even if you do not agree that the goal is a legitimate one. Whether or not we should attempt to transfer wealth from one group to another is a normative issue.

Government policy is a topic worth understanding; you will probably pay close to half of your lifetime income to the government. You will be taxed on almost everything you do, so it's worth consideration. This is the first section where government policy is the primary focus.

- **Rationing Mechanism**
    - The market price is a rationing mechanism
        - society faces scarcity, and must somehow allocate the resources to certain people, necessarily excluding others, both on the production and consumption side of the market
            - input resources (land, labor, capital, and managerial skill) are allocated to the firms with

the lowest cost of production, i.e., those in the lower left part of the S curve

- final goods are allocated to the consumers who expect to get the most benefit from consumption, i.e., those in the upper left part of the D curve

o If we do not use the price mechanism to allocate scarce resources, then *some other criterion must be used*

- for each price control case, think of what criteria will ultimately allocate the scarce resources
- will that be better or fairer than the price mechanism?
- we're going to take for granted the goal of these policies, though they could be easily argued against

- **Price Ceilings**
  - o A price ceiling is a law that makes market transactions above a particular price illegal
    - generally implemented with the stated intent of helping consumers
    - for a price ceiling to be effective (or binding), it must be set <u>below Pe</u>
      - don't be confused; it might look like a "floor"
      - see Figure G.1
    - a certain outcome of all effective price ceilings is a shortage (Qd>Qs)
    - a price ceiling may encourage wasteful consumption, by pushing price down
    - the number of mutually beneficial, voluntary transactions (Q_T) <u>must fall</u> as a result of a price ceiling (that's bad)

- **Price Floors**
  - o These make transactions below a certain price illegal
    - goal is to help producers; but harms consumers

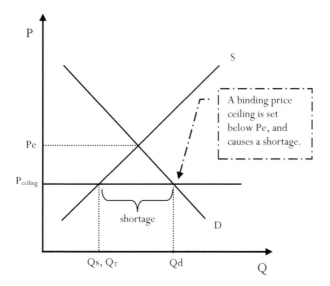

Figure G.1. Binding price ceilings create shortages and reduce voluntary transactions

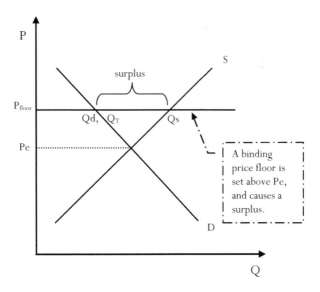

Figure G.2. Binding price floors create surpluses and reduce voluntary transactions

84

- to be effective (binding), the price floor must be set <u>above Pe</u>
  - don't be confused; it might look like a "ceiling"
  - see Figure G.2
- a certain outcome of all effective price floors is a surplus (Qs>Qd)
- a price floor encourages over production (a waste of resources), by pushing prices up
- again in this case, Q_T must fall as a result of this policy, relative to Pe

- **General Effects**
  - Recognize that these clearly reduce overall welfare in society since they reduce Q_T
    - someone must be worse off, since transactions are prevented
    - there will be unsatisfied people in the market now
      - with a price floor, designed to benefit *sellers*, there won't be enough buyers (Qs>Qd), so sellers are unsatisfied
      - with a price ceiling, designed to benefit *buyers*, there won't be enough sellers (Qd>Qs), so buyers are unsatisfied
  - Price controls bring unintended side-effects
  - If these policies harm society overall, why does government impose them?
    - people tend not to understand what happens when these laws are enacted
    - they tend to sympathize with the politicians' arguments in favor of the policies
  - Lobbying incentives are very important in explaining why we have price controls (as well as many other laws)
    - the harm from the policy is usually <u>dispersed</u> among a lot of people, so they have no real incentive to lobby against the policy

- the benefits from the policy is usually <u>concentrated</u>, and that group has a very strong incentive to lobby in favor of the policy

- **Steps for Analyzing Policy Impacts**
  - Determine the intent or goal of the policy
    - how do the politicians sell it?
  - Analyze the policy to determine its likely economic effects
  - Determine whether the policy achieves its goal
  - What are possible alternatives that may more effectively achieve the goals of the policy?

- **Rent Control Laws**
  - Price ceiling on apartment rental rates
  - The intent is to make housing affordable for college students and poor people
  - These tend to be popular in college towns and in large cities
    - would it be good for Charleston?
    - just because they're popular, does that mean they're helpful?
  - Rent controls cause shortages
    - more applicants than available apartments
    - will the students and the poor end up with the apartments?
    - key deposits, bribes, discrimination, poor maintenance, etc.
    - see the 2003 HUD ad on housing discrimination[23]
  - A better alternative would be direct (cash) subsidies; dormitories

---

[23] https://www.youtube.com/watch?v=YXxCYkquRYs

- **Anti-Price Gouging Laws**
  - Usually implemented during declared states of emergency[24]
  - Prices for water, lumber, gas, etc., may go up after a natural disaster
  - Price gouging in SC means that after a state of emergency is declared, the price of a good or service is "much higher" than the average price 30 days prior to the state of emergency[25]
    - Ex: Charleston price increases after Hurricane Hugo: bags of ice went up to $10; plywood went up to $200 per sheet; gas went up to $11/gallon
    - Charleston mayor signed law punishing price gouging (30 days in jail, $200 fine)
  - After Katrina, a Kentucky man bought 19 generators and drove to Mississippi to sell generators for twice what he paid
    - he was arrested and held by police for 4 days, and the generators were confiscated and never got used by hurricane victims
  - A price ceiling will create a shortage; who gets water?
    - whoever waits in line?
      - a person wanting to refill the swimming pool or build a tree house is just as likely to get supplies as a person needing drinking water or lumber to repair his roof
    - by lottery or quota?
  - Allowing the P to ↑ freely is the *best* policy, because it comes with two important incentive effects[26]

---

[24] The examples below are from Gwartney et al., *Economics: Private and Public Choice* 13th edition (2010, pp. 84-85).

[25] See http://www.consumer.sc.gov. Search for keyword "price gouging," click on the first result and a pdf opens.

[26] See John Stossel, "In Praise of Price Gouging" (2005)

- consumers have a higher incentive to conserve the water since it's more expensive; don't refill your swimming pool yet...
- suppliers have a strong profit incentive to get more water in stock quickly
  - Suppose after a flood, Lowe's increases its stock of water pumps without raising prices, while Home Depot doesn't increase stocks?
  - What should you send to help natural disaster victims?

Figure G.3. During the flooding in South Carolina in October 2015, Lowe's had a large stock of water pumps and other flood-related supplies and equipment – at regular price

- **Outrage Over Pharmaceuticals**[27]
  - In September 2015 there was widespread outrage over a young entrepreneur whose company bought the production rights of the drug "Daraprim"
    - the drug has been unchanged for 62 years
    - about 2,000 people take the drug

---

[27] This discussion is based on a 2015 article in the *New York Times*, http://www.nytimes.com/2015/09/21/business/a-huge-overnight-increase-in-a-drugs-price-raises-protests.html?_r=0.

- the price of the drug was promptly increased from $13.50 to $750 per pill
  - Hillary Clinton said, "Price gouging like this in the specialty drug market is outrageous."
  - One month later, a competitor began offering a similar pill for just $1 per pill[28]
    - a great example of how profit attracts new producers

- **Gas Price Ceiling**
  - These have been enacted several times in the U.S., with the predictable result of shortages
    - waiting in line is a "deadweight loss" – a cost to consumers not offset by gains to someone else
    - the higher price is a transfer of wealth, but the waiting cost is a societal loss
    - why do gas prices jump when there's trouble in the Middle East?

- **Agriculture Price Supports**
  - Price floors on agricultural products are very popular; consider one for milk
  - Political argument might be that farmers are important in America's history, and markets are "unfair" to them
  - A price floor creates a surplus
    - government must guarantee that farmers can sell their milk at the price floor price, otherwise they have inventory they can't sell
    - government must buy and destroy the surplus milk, or otherwise take it off the market
    - this is a very inefficient way to transfer wealth to farmers – creating an incentive to overproduce; something else cannot now be produced
  - Why not just send them a check each year?
    - why subsidize them in the first place?

---

[28] http://fortune.com/2015/10/23/turing-daraprim-cheap-alternative/

- **Minimum Wage Laws**
  - These are very politically popular
    - goal is to help poor, unskilled, uneducated workers
  - Federal minimum wage is $7.25, since July 2009
    - many states have minimums above the federal level
    - cities can implement higher wages
    - if a state has no minimum wage law, the federal still applies

Table G.1. State minimum wage law rates, as of July 2018

State	Min. Wage	State	Min. Wage
Alabama	none	Nebraska	$9.00
Alaska	$9.84	Nevada	$8.25
Arizona	$10.50	N. Hampshire	none
Arkansas	$8.50	New Jersey	$8.60
California	$11.00	New Mexico	$7.50
Colorado	$10.20	New York	$10.40
Connecticut	$10.10	N. Carolina	$7.25
Delaware	$8.25	North Dakota	$7.25
Florida	$8.25	Ohio	$8.30
Georgia	$5.15	Oklahoma	$7.25
Hawaii	$10.10	Oregon	$10.75
Idaho	$7.25	Pennsylvania	$7.25
Illinois	$8.25	Rhode Island	$10.10
Indiana	$7.25	**S. Carolina**	**none**
Iowa	$7.25	South Dakota	$8.85
Kansas	$7.25	Tennessee	none
Kentucky	$7.25	Texas	$7.25
Louisiana	none	Utah	$7.25
Maine	$10.00	Vermont	$10.50
Maryland	$10.10	Virginia	$7.25
Massachusetts	$11.00	Washington	$11.50
Michigan	$9.25	West Virginia	$8.75
Minnesota	$9.65	Wisconsin	$7.25
Mississippi	none	Wyoming	$5.15
Missouri	$7.85	D. C.	$13.25
Montana	$8.30		

Source: http://www.ncsl.org/research/labor-and-employment/state-minimum-wage-chart.aspx#Table

- o CA, MA, and NY have scheduled increases until they reach $15.00
- o Why not raise it to $25 or $30, or $100?
- o Minimum wage laws are price floors on wages paid to "unskilled labor"
    - creates a surplus of labor (unemployment) because there are more job applicants than jobs
        - are the least skilled, experienced and educated people (the people most in need of help) the ones likely to get the jobs?
    - a surplus of labor means that employers can discriminate on non-price basis
    - workers are replaced with capital (see Figure G.4)
        - fast food workers have gone on strike to get higher wages
        - at Charleston airport, most parking lanes are "express" – no humans
        - at Atlanta airport, trash compactors replace some workers
- o As with the dairy case, government must "buy" the surplus – it has unemployment insurance programs for those who can't find jobs
    - it would be better to offer cash subsidies or subsidized education or job training
    - there's debate over whether it really creates any significant unemployment
- o Should we have a lower minimum wage for teens?
    - Obama's past economic advisor Larry Summers has endorsed this in the past
    - only 1% of full-time workers earn the minimum wage; 90% of them are age 16-20
        - maybe a crappy job would be a strong incentive to stay in school
        - at least these people could get some job experience

Figure G.4. Examples of capital replacing labor: a kiosk at McDonald's in Amsterdam, a trash compactor at the Atlanta airport, and parking pay station in Asheville, NC

o   Henry Hazlitt had a good discussion of minimum wage laws (p. 135):

"The first thing that happens when a law is passed that no one shall be paid less than [$400] for a forty-hour week is that no one who is not worth [$400] a week to an employer will be employed at all. *You cannot make a man worth a given amount by making it illegal for anyone to offer him anything less.* You merely deprive him of the right to earn the amount that his abilities and situation would permit him to earn, while you deprive the community even of the moderate services that he is capable of rendering. In brief, for a low wage you substitute unemployment. You do harm all around..."

- if the minimum wage is $400 per week, and we offer $300 per week in unemployment benefits, we're asking people to work for $100 per week
- states with higher employment benefits have higher rates of unemployment, and individuals tend to be unemployed longer

LECTURE H: ELASTICITY

   Now that we've developed the basics of supply, demand, and price determination, we'll look in a bit more detail about what the slopes of the curves imply. "Elasticity" is the responsiveness or sensitivity of one variable to changes in another variable. While this section is rather short and slightly technical, there are some interesting applications for these concepts.

- **Price Elasticity of Demand**
  - "Elasticity" is the sensitivity of one variable to changes in another variable
    - in terms of S & D, it means the slope of the curve
  - The price elasticity of demand, $\varepsilon_d = \dfrac{\%\Delta Qd}{\%\Delta P}$
    - this number will always be negative, so we simply drop the sign
    - demand is "elastic" if $\varepsilon_d > 1$, which means consumers are very sensitive to changes in P
    - demand is "inelastic" if $\varepsilon_d < 1$, which means that consumers are not very sensitive to changes in P
    - demand is "unit elastic" if $\varepsilon_d = 1$
    - Ex: insulin probably has a very inelastic or steep D curve
      - for a 10% price increase, there is probably a very small decrease in Qd, maybe 1%
        - in this example, $\varepsilon_d = 1/10 = 0.10$, which is less than 1
      - people who take insulin are not responsive to the price change because they *need* insulin
    - Ex: Exxon gasoline probably has a very elastic or flat D curve
      - for just a 5% increase in price, suppose they see a 20% decrease in sales; then $\varepsilon_d = 20/5 = 4$; since 4 > 1, it's elastic

- people buying gas are very responsive to prices because they can easily go buy it across the street where it's cheaper
  - Ex: Coke will have more elastic demand than "soft drinks" generally
- o The "midpoint method" or "arc elasticity" is the best way to make the elasticity calculation
  - % change is calculated as the "difference/ average"
  - if old price is 5 and new price is 7, % change is calculated $2/6 = 0.333$
- o Determinants of ε_d
  - number of close substitutes (more $\Rightarrow$ more elastic)
    - a particular brand will have more elastic D than the good generally
  - necessity versus luxury (luxury goods $\Rightarrow$ more elastic D)
  - time horizon (longer time $\Rightarrow$ more elastic D)
  - proportion of price to income (higher $\Rightarrow$ more elastic)

- **Price Changes and Total Revenue**
  - o The ε_d is important information for businesses that must decide which P to charge
    - you can't simply think that total revenue (TR) will increase if you just raise P
      - what if people quit buying the product?
  - o Figure H.1 illustrates the effect of price changes on TR, in the case of inelastic D
    - as a result of the 200% price increase, there is a 33% reduction in Qd ($\varepsilon_d=33/200=0.17$; but if price had dropped from \$6 to \$2, $\varepsilon_d=50/67=0.75$)
      - using the midpoint method, ε_d $=(2/5)/(4/4)=0.4/1=0.4$ (inelastic)

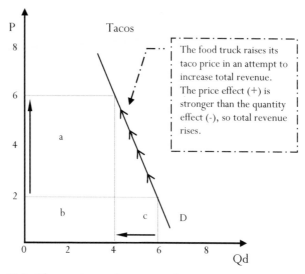

Figure H.1. Change in total revenue due to an increase in P, with inelastic demand

- notice that if the taco truck raises price from $2 to $6 each, it receives more money per taco, and they don't lose too many sales
  - TR before the P↑ was b+c ($12=6 x $2)
  - after the ΔP, TR is a+b ($24=4 x $6)
  - to increase TR (with inelastic demand), ↑P
  - if D is very flat, then TR ↑ when P↓

- **The Federal "War on Drugs"**
  - Mr. Mackey's disclaimer: "Drugs are bad, mkay."
    - discussing a policy such as drug legalization is not the same as advocating drug use
    - drug use may, in fact, be harmful; but it does not follow that a legal ban on drug use will minimize harms
  - The market for "drugs" probably has very inelastic D
    - some users become addicted
    - others take drugs even when it's illegal, so they probably don't care much about money price

- o The government focuses on capturing suppliers
  - this increases the cost of supplying drugs, so S falls
  - the result is a huge increase in P, but not much of a decrease in Q
  - do you think this encourages the more or less violent dealers to remain in the business?
    - if you already face a life sentence for dealing, what's the marginal penalty for killing your competitors too?
  - why focus on the S side rather than D side?
- o Drug use in the U.S. is very prevalent, even after spending hundreds of billions over 30 years
  - marijuana use rate is much higher in the U.S. (36%) than in countries that have decriminalized
    - marijuana has been tolerated in Holland for decades (20% prevalence rate)
    - in 2001 Portugal decriminalized all drug use (7% marijuana use prevalence rate)[29]
  - the war on drugs tends to make the drugs more potent, as dealers/users want to keep bulk down (less likely to get caught with more potent drugs)
- o Federal government classification of drugs, research, and propaganda are political and questionable
  - research on ecstasy or MDMA[30]
  - commercials about marijuana & auto accidents[31]
  - DEA lists marijuana as a Schedule I drug[32]:

---

[29] For an analysis of the Portugal experience with decriminalization, see http://www.tdpf.org.uk/blog/drug-decriminalisation-portugal-setting-record-straight.

[30] A very interesting documentary aired on ABC in 2005. It described the development of MDMA and how the federal government handled it. The scientific understanding of the drug has certainly advanced since then. If interested, see http://www.youtube.com/watch?v=DNpFqJcJcps.

[31] http://www.youtube.com/watch?v=MKCYDrur_WI

[32] http://www.dea.gov/druginfo/ds.shtml

"Schedule I drugs, substances, or chemicals are defined as drugs with no currently accepted medical use and a high potential for abuse. Schedule I drugs are the most dangerous drugs of all the drug schedules with potentially severe psychological or physical dependence."

- Ex: heroin, LSD, *marijuana*, MDMA
  - Marijuana enforcement has been relaxed since 2009
    - in 2009 Obama ordered the DEA not to raid medical marijuana shops in states where they are legal (according to state government)
    - in 2013 Attorney General Eric Holder moved to stop seeking mandatory sentences for nonviolent drug offenses
    - in 2014 the DEA requested that the FDA study marijuana, in considering a downgrade from Schedule 1
      - the FDA argued that there is no accepted medical use in treatment in the US, so the DEA decided to keep it in Schedule I (August 2016)
      - public choice would have predicted this: they have their turf to protect
    - in 2015 three U.S. senators introduced a bill to stop prosecution of medical marijuana use, and to re-classify marijuana as a Schedule II drug[33]

---

[33] https://www.congress.gov/bill/114th-congress/senate-bill/683

98

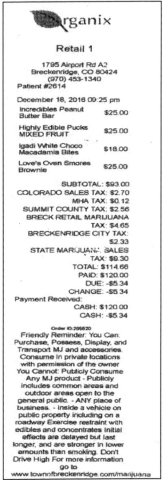

Figure H.3. A receipt for edibles sold in Colorado

o State governments have moved toward legalization or decriminalization of marijuana, despite federal law[34]
  ▪ around 30 states have medical marijuana laws
  ▪ about 16 have "decriminalized" marijuana
    • still illegal, but it's an administrative offense, not criminal offense (small fines)
o as of 2018, AK, CA, CO, DC, OR, MA, ME, NV, and WA have legal recreational use
o Different countries (e.g., Portugal, Holland) have different, more effective strategies

---

[34] See http://norml.org for information on state-level marijuana laws.

- enforcement (USA)[35]
- education
- treatment
  - Trump appointed Sen. Jeff Sessions (R-AL) as Attorney General
    - Sessions has said, "Good people don't smoke marijuana"
    - one April 2017 headline said, "Jeff Sessions says he's 'surprised' Americans aren't embracing his anti-marijuana stance"
    - he appears to want to re-escalate the failed "war on drugs"[36]
      - in May 2017, Sessions reversed AG Holder's 2013 policy of not seeking mandatory minimum sentences for non-violent drug offenses
      - Trump has attacked Sessions, but he's still AG

- **Elasticity of Supply**
  - This concept is similar to ε_d except it deals with supply:
    $$\varepsilon_s = \frac{\%\Delta Qs}{\%\Delta P}$$
  - The main determinant for ε_s is the time period
    - longer time, easier to change production quantities
    - labor contracts might affect production
    - apartment S is fairly steep; factory output is flatter

- **Other Applications of Elasticity**
  - Later we'll analyze excise taxes, relying on an understanding of elasticity of supply and demand

---

[35] For an interesting video on drug policy, see https://www.youtube.com/watch?v=wJUXLqNHCaI.

[36] For a discussion of harsher sentences for drug trafficking, see https://www.youtube.com/watch?v=3uyn8QwOJ7c.

LECTURE I: EXCISE TAXES AND DEADWEIGHT LOSSES

Excise taxes are very common, and their effects are interesting. Although the tax is legally imposed on either the buyer or seller, the actual burden of the tax has nothing to do with the legal burden.

An efficient tax would not change behavior at all. An example would be a lump-sum tax, say of $1,000 per year per U.S. citizen. These taxes do not change behavior, and so they are efficient. However, they are extremely *regressive*. That is, the tax places a heavier burden on a poor person than on a rich person. This is because $1,000 is a much greater proportion of a poor person's income. For this reason, among others, lump-sum taxes are not as popular as excise and other types of taxes.

Excise taxes are inefficient because they are placed only on certain goods. As a result, they tend to distort behavior by discouraging consumption of those goods. The reduction in these transactions causes losses in CS and PS – reductions in social wealth.

Our analysis in this lecture is relatively complicated, but it is useful to analyze tax revenues and related "deadweight losses."

- **Excise Taxes**
  - Everyone is familiar with the sales tax; it's 6% in SC
    - Charleston County adds 3%
    - this was just increased from 2.5% in May 2017, thanks to voters
  - Excise taxes are similar to sales taxes, but are imposed on specific items, not all items
    - Ex: City of Charleston adds a 2% hospitality tax on prepared meals and beverages (this is why you pay a 11% tax at restaurants)
    - Ex: SC adds a 5% liquor tax at bars & restaurants
      - total tax on your liquor drink at the bar: 16%!
  - Most excise taxes we'll look at are set at the state-level, but there are also federal excise taxes

o   "Sin taxes" are taxes on alcohol, cigarettes, gambling, etc., and are often very high
  ▪ states set their own cigarette taxes
    • SC increased its cigarette tax from 7¢ to 57¢, on July 1, 2010
    • goal is to raise revenue and deter smoking, especially for young people
  ▪ the federal cigarette tax was raised from 39¢/pack to $1.01/pack in April 2009

Table I.1. State excise taxes on cigarettes (2018)

State	Tax (¢)	Rank	State	Tax (¢)	Rank
Alabama	67.5	40	Nebraska	64	41
Alaska	200	15	Nevada	180	21
Arizona	200	15	N. Hampshire	178	22
Arkansas	115	34	New Jersey	270	10
California	287	9	New Mexico	166	25
Colorado	84	38	New York	435	1
Connecticut	435	1	**NYC**	**585**	
Delaware	210	14	N. Carolina	45	47
Florida	133.9	30	North Dakota	44	48
Georgia	37	49	Ohio	160	26
Hawaii	320	5	Oklahoma	103	36
Idaho	57	45	Oregon	133	31
Illinois	198	20	Pennsylvania	260	11
Indiana	99.5	37	Rhode Island	425	3
Iowa	136	29	**S. Carolina**	**57**	**45**
Kansas	129	32	South Dakota	153	27
Kentucky	60	43	Tennessee	62	42
Louisiana	108	35	Texas	141	28
Maine	200	15	Utah	170	23
Maryland	200	15	Vermont	308	6
Massachusetts	351	4	Virginia	30	50
Michigan	200	15	Washington	302.5	8
Minnesota	304	7	West Virginia	120	33
Mississippi	68	39	Wisconsin	252	12
Missouri	17	51	Wyoming	60	43
Montana	170	23	D. C.	250	13

Source: http://www.taxadmin.org/assets/docs/Research/Rates/cigarette.pdf. Tax rates as of January 1, 2018.

- ○ Gasoline is taxed in every state (from around 15-55¢ per gallon)
    - the federal tax is 18.3¢/gal.
    - SC state tax increased on July 1, 2017, after a few years of debate
        - now 20.75¢/gal., to increase 2¢ each July 1 until it reaches 28.75¢
        - Alaska has the lowest tax; SC is second lowest
- ○ Luxury items are often a target for excise taxes
    - President Bill Clinton threatened a 100% luxury car tax back in 1995 during a trade dispute with Japan[37]
    - A 10% tax on yachts priced over $100K in 1990 was estimated to cost thousands of jobs[38]

- **Tax Burden (or Incidence)**
    - ○ Usually the government puts the legal responsibility for remitting the tax money on the <u>sellers</u>
        - there are relatively few sellers compared to consumers – easier to keep track of the money
        - public perception that sellers are "rich," and they should pay the tax
    - ○ The application of an excise tax to our market model is very simple if you understand what the S and D curves represent
    - ○ If an excise tax (τ) is placed on the suppliers, then it affects the S curve like any other additional cost would
        - S would shift vertically higher (S falls)
        - to be willing to supply the same Q after the tax is imposed, the seller would need to receive the original selling price, plus the tax amount, from the consumer

---

[37] http://articles.latimes.com/1995-05-17/news/mn-2817_1_white-house

[38] http://www.nytimes.com/1992/02/07/business/falling-tax-would-lift-all-yachts.html

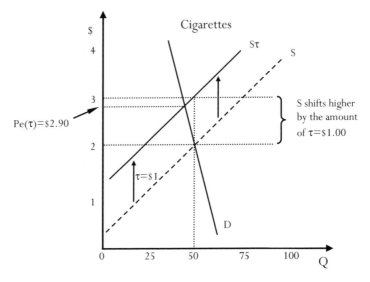

Figure I.1. An excise tax with a statutory burden on sellers

- ▪ Figure I.1 illustrates a $1 per-pack tax on cigarettes
  - ● original Pe is $2.00; new Pe is $2.90
  - ● effectively, 90¢ of the tax comes from consumers' pockets, since they now pay more
  - ● sellers can shift most of the tax to consumers
- ○ Relative tax burden is determined by the relative elasticities of supply and demand
  - ▪ whoever is less sensitive to price changes will bear more of the tax
  - ▪ the actual tax burden does <u>not</u> depend on the <u>statutory burden</u> (who's legally required to pay the tax)
- ○ To find the tax burdens we compare the new situation (with τ) to the old one (without τ)
  - ▪ Figure I.2 illustrates "sliding the tax wedge in from the left"
- ○ The consumer's burden is the new price they pay (Pb) minus the original equilibrium price (before τ)
  - ▪ here it's $2.90 – $2.00, or **90¢**

- The seller's burden is what's left (it's a $1 tax per pack, and the consumer bears 90¢), or **10¢**
  - it's the new price they receive from consumers ($2.90), minus the $1 tax paid to government, leaving sellers with $1.90 after the tax ($P_s$)
  - since they used to get $2.00 and now they get $1.90, the sellers are paying 10¢ of the tax
- How exactly does the relative tax burden depend on the elasticities of supply and demand?
  - the steeper curve will carry a heavier burden
  - try drawing other examples similar to Figure I.2, to convince yourself how this works

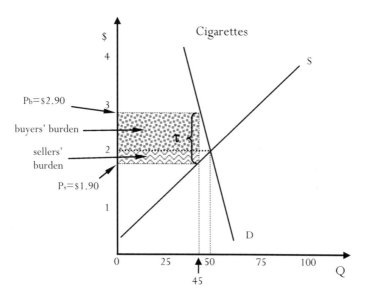

Figure I.2. Analysis of actual excise tax burden

- Finally, consider the FICA tax in your paycheck
  - the "Federal Insurance Contribution Act" is to fund Medicare and the Social Security program
  - this is split; the employee and employer each pay half of the 15.3% tax (7.65% each)

106

- 6.2% social security tax, on first $128,400 income (for 2018)[39]
    - 1.45% Medicare tax on entire salary
  - does the 50-50 split between employer & employee really matter?
    - supply of labor is probably more inelastic than demand for labor
      - employees end up bearing most of the employment tax

- **Deadweight Losses (DWL)**
  - A deadweight loss represents a loss of societal wealth
    - loss to one group/individual that's not simultaneously gained by someone else
    - a tax is different –a transfer of wealth
    - DWL is lost CS and PS because fewer transactions will take place
  - Figure I.3 illustrates the DWL from the cigarette tax we were discussing above
    - the size of the DWL will depend on the ε_d and ε_s
    - what happens when either becomes more elastic or inelastic?

- **Relatively Efficient & Inefficient Excise Taxes**
  - The sizes of the tax revenue rectangle and the DWL triangle both depend on ε_d and ε_s
    - Figure I.4 shows the same per-unit tax as in Figure I.3, but just with a more elastic demand curve
    - more elastic S or D, then lower tax revenue and larger DWL, *ceteris paribus*
  - Given S & D, what happens when the size of the per-unit tax is varied?
    - a very large tax may result in lower tax revenue, if the number of transactions falls by a large amount

---

[39] http://www.ssa.gov/oact/cola/cbb.html

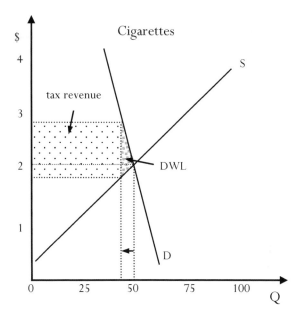

Figure I.3. Deadweight loss from an excise tax on cigarettes

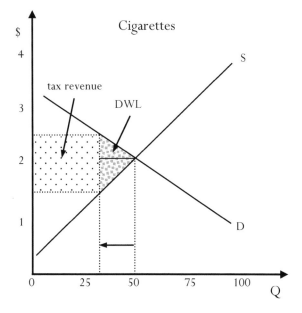

Figure I.4. The DWL triangle increases in size when S or D becomes more elastic

LECTURE J: INTERNATIONAL TRADE POLICY

This section is an extension of Lectures B, F and I; it discusses trade policy using the concepts of CS, PS, and DWL. In the development of the Ricardian trade model we learned why trade benefits both parties involved. (At least both parties must expect to benefit, otherwise they wouldn't agree to the trade. This does not preclude their expectations being wrong.)

Economists argue that "free trade," or trade free of government interference or restrictions, is the best policy – even if it's unilateral. One might wonder, then, if trade is so good, why would government ever want to prevent it? The answer to the question is the same one that explains much of government policy: to give favors to one group at the expense of others.

In the case of international trade, government imposes many barriers, including tariffs, quotas, and other regulations affecting imported products.

In 2018, President Trump began following through on his campaign promises to shake-up trade. As of summer, he had imposed tariffs on imported steel and aluminum, and washing machines. In July, he continued to make threats to restrict imports. He tweeted, "Tariffs are the greatest!" He has also proposed a bailout for farmers who are expected to be harmed because of retaliatory tariffs from China and the European Union.

Trump appears to believe that his strategy of imposing trade restrictions, particularly tariffs, will eventually lead to more open markets, or a greater ability of U.S. manufacturers and farmers to sell their products abroad. On July 25, Trump announced that he had reached an agreement with the EU to seek zero tariffs, subsidies, and non-tariff barriers on all non-auto industries. It will be interesting to watch to see if Trump's strategy works. One thing is certain: Trump is taking a very different approach to trade than many of his predecessors!

Before studying this section, it might be helpful for you to review consumer and producer surplus. These are key variables that we will use to evaluate the welfare impacts of trade restrictions.

- **Landsburg, "The Iowa Car Crop (Ch. 21)**
  - A nice short story that illustrates that trade is merely a form of technology
  - He suggests that much of the opposition to trade might simply be an irrational dislike for foreigners
  - There is a strong belief among laymen that international trade is a "win-lose" game
    - but we've already shown that trade is win-win, a "positive sum game"
    - yet, it's easy to see why people would misunderstand
    - "sweatshops" and "outsourcing" as political issues
  - Is trade a "jobs" issue?
    - no; trade has no real effect on the <u>level</u> of employment
    - but it does affect the <u>distribution</u> of employment across industries
    - if you want government to help one industry, you can, but you must harm another industry to do it
      - don't forget this when you hear lobbyists arguing for a policy to help their industry

- **Modeling International Trade Restrictions**
  - We can use the supply-demand model to investigate the effects of trade restrictions
    - recall the concepts of CS and PS
    - in the model the S and D curves are "domestic"
    - we assume the country is "small" so actors don't have any effect on the world price (P_W)
      - P_W may differ from $P_{No\ Trade}$
  - Moving from self-sufficiency to free trade
    - compare the initial case to the new case (Figure J.1)
      - CS and PS changes; overall (net) change
  - When $P_W > P_{NT}$, what happens if you go from "no trade" to free trade?
    - there will be excess domestic supply

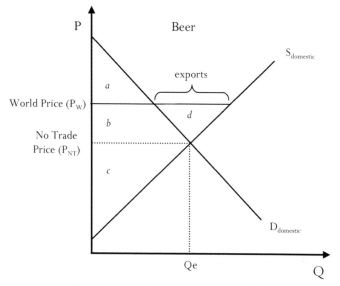

Figure J.1. Welfare effect of eliminating a trade ban ($P_W > P_{NT}$)

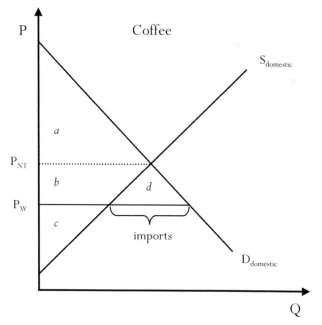

Figure J.2. Welfare effect of eliminating a trade ban ($P_W < P_{NT}$)

- since the world market is in equilibrium, our excess domestic supply is exported
- PS↑, and CS↓, but the overall (net) effect is positive
  - What about when $P_W<P_{NT}$? (Figure J.2)
    - there will be excess domestic demand; we import
    - PS↓, CS↑, and total surplus ↑

- **Import Tariffs**
  - We can use the same basic model to analyze the effects of an import tariff
  - A tariff is simply a tax on imported goods, paid by the importing firms to the domestic government
    - for import tariffs, $P_W<P_{NT}$, so there are imports
    - the tax effectively increases P_W (to $P_{W+\tau}$) in the country imposing the tariff
    - the tariff causes an increase in domestic production of 20 units (from 40 to 60),

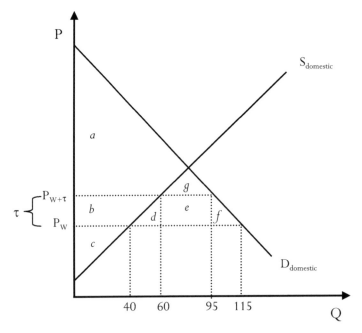

Figure J.3. Welfare effects of a tariff of τ per unit

- a decrease in domestic consumption of 20 (from 115 to 95),
- and a decrease in imports of 40 (from 75 to 35, calculated 115-40 to 95-60)
  - What happens to each group?
    - increase in PS (*b*)
    - increase in tariff revenue (*e*)
    - decrease in CS (*b*+*d*+*e*+*f*)
    - so the net effect is a DWL of (*d*+*f*)

- **Import Quotas**
  - These are limits on the quantities of imported goods
  - They can have effects equivalent to tariffs
    - but quotas are generally worse since quantity imported cannot increase
    - P is more likely to rise under a quota than a tariff
  - Overall the welfare effect from quotas is similar to that from tariffs
    - there's a DWL

- **Bureaucratic Waste and Trade Regulations**
  - Consider how much effort (time, money) is put into developing and enforcing trade restrictions
    - See the U.S. International Trade Commission website for a glimpse at the complexity of tariffs
    - www.usitc.gov, click "Tariff Search Tool", and search for your favorite product
      - Schedule 1 is for "most favored nations"; 2 is for non-WTO countries
  - Tariffs raise little money for the government
  - Enforcement costs are significant
    - people on docks; paperwork; lobbying

- **Arguments Typically Used to Support Trade Restrictions**
  - ○ Trump is a protectionist, and has been sympathetic to restricting imports
  - ○ Most are simply lobbying strategies by domestic producers who want government to restrict competition from foreign firms
    - national defense
      - this one is perhaps reasonable in limited cases
      - but everyone from oil, steel, autos, tries to use this argument
      - Trump has used this as a justification for imports on steel and aluminum[40]
    - infant industry
    - anti-dumping
    - patriotism ("buy American!")
      - Ex: before the 2012 summer Olympics, it was discovered that the U.S. athlete's outfits were made in China; Nevada Senator Harry Reid suggested that the uniforms should be burned and replaced with U.S.-made uniforms[41]
    - cheap foreign labor
      - but wage rates reflect productivity
    - "unfair" trade practices
      - government subsidies
      - lax environmental or labor standards in the other country

---

[40] https://piie.com/commentary/op-eds/trump-has-announced-massive-aluminum-and-steel-tariffs

[41] https://www.washingtonpost.com/blogs/2012-heavy-medal-london/post/us-olympic-uniforms-spark-fury-in-congress/2012/07/13/gJQABvJmhW_blog.html?utm_term=.d01a0f473f51

- **Cost of Jobs Saved by Protectionism**
  - In 2002 the Federal Reserve Bank of Dallas published estimates of the cost per U.S. job saved by import restrictions[42]
    - average cost is *$231,000 per worker per year*, in 2002 dollars
  - Overall, these restrictions cost consumers $100 billion per year ($320 per U.S. resident)
  - Consider U.S. sugar jobs, which cost $826,000 to protect each year (Table J.1)
    - more recent analysis suggests the sugar quota costs U.S. consumers $3-4 billion per year[43]
    - it'd be more efficient to just write those workers a check and let them stay home
  - Understand the politics of "import protection" versus "wealth transfer"

"The High Costs of Protectionism"

The average cost of protecting an American job is $231,289, in the 20 industries listed below. The total cost to U.S. consumers is over $100 billion annually, over $300 per person per year. Aside from causing higher prices for protected goods, import restrictions also cause higher prices in "downstream" industries (that use the protected products as input resources).

These data are reproduced from the Dallas Fed's 2002 *Annual Report*. The estimated costs would be much higher now, if the data were adjusted for inflation.

---

[42] From the Federal Reserve Bank of Dallas, 2002 Annual report, "The Fruits of Free Trade," available at https://www.dallasfed.org/fed/annual/~/media/documents/fed/annual/2002/ar02.pdf.

[43] http://www.aei.org/publication/big-sugar-costs-us-consumers-3-7-billion-every-year-in-higher-prices-and-has-killed-127000-jobs-since-1997/; for a more detailed analysis, see http://www.usnews.com/opinion/economic-intelligence/2014/09/05/sugar-price-supports-have-hidden-costs-for-economy-consumers.

Table J.1. Estimated cost, jobs saved by trade restrictions (2002)

	Protected industry	Jobs saved	Total cost (millions $)	Annual cost per job saved
1	Benzenoid chem.	216	$297	$1,376,435
2	Luggage	226	290	1,285,078
3	Softwood lumber	605	632	1,044,271
4	Sugar	2261	1868	826,104
5	Polyethylene resins	298	242	812,928
6	Dairy products	2378	1630	685,323
7	Frozen conc. OJ	609	387	635,103
8	Ball bearings	146	88	603,368
9	Maritime services	4411	2522	571,668
10	Ceramic tiles	347	191	551,367
11	Machine tools	1556	746	479,452
12	Ceramic articles	418	140	335,876
13	Women's handbags	773	204	263,535
14	Canned tuna	390	100	257,640
15	Glassware	1477	366	247,889
16	Apparel/textiles	168,786	33,629	199,241
17	Peanuts	397	74	187,223
18	Rubber footwear	1701	286	168,312
19	Women's non-athletic footwear	3702	518	139,800
20	Costume jewelry	1067	142	132,870
Totals		*191,764*	*$44,352*	
Weighted average cost per job saved				*$231,289*

Source: *Annual Report*, Federal Reserve Bank of Dallas (2002, p. 19)

LECTURE K: MARKET FAILURES

In the first part of the course, we've concentrated on markets, how they work, and the effects of government policies. These discussions assumed that markets were "perfectly competitive." In most cases, markets lead to relatively efficient outcomes.

There are some situations, however, in which free markets do *not* lead to efficient outcomes. One example would be a monopoly (a market with just one seller), which restricts quantity and raises price above what the competitive market would be. Two other examples are externalities and public goods, the primary subjects of this lecture.

We'll discuss the issues along with theoretical methods of "solving" the problems. Although these solutions may be difficult, if not impossible, to implement in the real world, the policy implemented should be designed to approximate the theoretical solutions as closely as possible.

The material in this lecture represents perhaps the most interesting policy issues that we cover in the class.

- **Common Property Ownership**
  - When everyone owns something, no one owns it
  - Look at the roadside, or a public restroom for example; no one has the incentive to take care of these
  - Air, rivers, some bodies of water, etc., are not owned
    - it is the lack of private property rights that leads to externalities problems (especially the negative ones)
    - think about elephants in Africa vs. cows (ivory vs. beef); what explains why one is near extinction while the other is not?
      - countries that have privatized elephants have higher growth rates[44]

---

[44] See McPherson and Nieswiadomy, "African Elephants: The Effect of Property Rights and Political Stability," *Contemporary Economic Policy* 18(1): 14-26 (2000).

- **Externalities**
  - o Rational behavior is the result of individuals considering the MC and MB of an action
    - ▪ but they're generally only concerned with the costs/benefits to *themselves*, not to others
    - ▪ when there are no externalities present, then the market looks like what we've studied in the first part of the course; everyone's happy

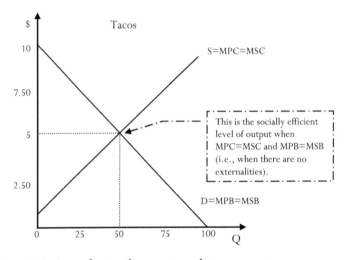

Figure K.1. A market with no externalities present

  - o An externality is a third-party or "external" effect of someone's action
    - ▪ these occur anytime MPB≠MSB or MPC≠MSC
      - • it's the standard model, but we distinguish between private "P" and social "S" in the above
    - ▪ for an overview, see *The Economist* article, "State and Market"
  - o Externalities can either be positive or negative, and can either be "production" externalities or "consumption" externalities
    - ▪ negative production externality: MSC>MPC
      - • Ex: pollution from factories

- Ex: the 2010 BP oil spill in the Gulf of Mexico
  - however, there was regulation of the industry... so is it only a "market" failure?
- negative consumption externality: MSB<MPB
  - think of it as a "negative social benefit"
  - Ex: cigarette smoking
  - Ex: violent video games, such as GTA
- positive production externality: MSC<MPC
  - Ex: technology spill-over
  - Ex: I-pad and applications
    - companies producing apps benefit from development of I-pad
- positive consumption externality: MSB>MPB
  - Ex: education
  - Ex: landscaping services
- Suppose the production of cars has toxic smoke as a byproduct
  - this represents a negative production externality
    - "marginal external damage" is shown in figure on p. 149
  - MSC>MPC
  - the damage caused by the smoke implies the total cost to society (the social cost) is greater than the production cost to the factory
    - but the factory doesn't take that cost into account when deciding how much to produce
  - see Figure K.2
    - the factory overproduces from a social perspective
    - but the socially efficient level of production is *not* zero, even though pollution is a bad thing
      - the socially efficient level of murder or theft probably isn't zero either
      - it would be far too costly to ensure zero of these bad things happened

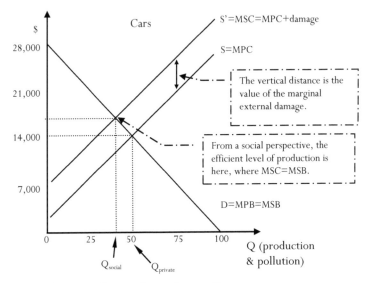

Figure K.2. Air pollution from the car factory represents a negative production externality

- **The Coase Theorem**
  - As long as property rights are defined, then the externalities problems disappear, assuming low bargaining costs
    - Ex: at the movie theater, turn off your phone!

Figure K.3. Signs at movie theaters asking you to shut up and not use your phone during the movie

- Ex: traffic at Lockwood and Bee St. downtown (see Figure K.4)

Figure K.4. The painting of the dashed white line through the intersection effectively assigned "property rights" to the lanes

- o This implies that a judge who is deciding a case involving a polluting factory and the harmed neighbors really "doesn't matter"
    - ▪ *the judge's decision is irrelevant, as long as the property right to the air is given to one party or the other*
    - ▪ consider two examples to see why we get this counter intuitive conclusion
        - • whether the judge sides with the factory or the neighbors, what amount of pollution results?
        - • see Figure K.5
- o This helps to emphasize the importance of private property rights for markets to work

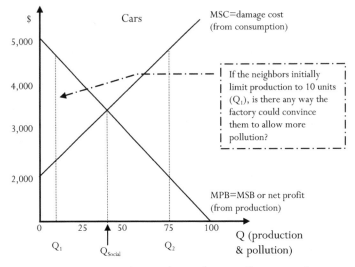

Figure K.5. Negotiations bring about the socially-optimal amount of pollution, whoever is given the property right to the air

- o The problem with this is that, generally, bargaining costs are not "low"
  - ▪ still, government could represent the neighbors, while an organization of factory owners represents the production side

- **Policy Options for Externalities**
  - o The key to solving externalities problems is to use government to make the MSB=MPB and MSC=MPC
    - ▪ this is called "internalizing" the externality
    - ▪ want to make the producer of the externality feel its effects
  - o You could try "moral suasion" – make people feel bad for harming others
    - ▪ this is not likely to be very successful
  - o Direct regulation is the most common policy, but it's not necessarily efficient
    - ▪ require scrubbers on smokestacks
    - ▪ force kids to go to school
    - ▪ no smoking in public places

- - drunk driving laws
  - 2017 ban on "tiny beads" in cosmetics[45]
  - o Pigouvian taxes and subsidies
    - for negative externalities, the creator is taxed for the damage caused to others
      - this causes the MPC curve to shift up to be equal to the MSC curve (if it's done properly)
      - on his own, the polluter will now choose to produce less (the socially optimal level?)
    - for positive consumption externalities, the behavior is subsidized
      - so the individual chooses to consume more
    - the problem is putting a dollar value on the externality – it's not easy
  - o Marketable permits (or "cap and trade") are perhaps the best method for allocating "pollution rights"
    - should these be allocated via auction or lottery?
    - should the permits be transferable or not?
    - these help ensure the scarce resource (the right to pollute) is allocated efficiently

- **Public Goods**
  - o These are defined very specifically, as having two characteristics
    - non-rival in consumption
    - non-excludable (prohibitively costly to exclude consumers)
      - then the MC of providing the good to an extra person may be zero
    - Ex: national defense, fireworks displays, radio/TV waves
  - o If a good isn't both non-rival and non-excludable, then it's otherwise classified (see Table K.1)

---

[45] http://www.rsc.org/chemistryworld/2016/01/us-bans-microbeads-personal-care-products

- private goods have neither characteristic
- "common resources" are rival but non-excludable
- "natural monopolies" are non-rival but excludable

Table K.1. Classification of goods

	Excludable	Non-excludable
Rival	*Private*	*Common resources*
Non-rival	*Natural monopoly*	*Pure public*

- o The "free rider" problem is the major reason government is called upon to provide public goods
  - if a good is non-excludable, then private firms cannot make people pay for using the product – so they aren't going to make a profit
  - the government can get around this by…taxing
- o Even though the government is called upon to provide public goods, it is difficult, if not impossible, for them to determine the socially optimal level of the goods
  - elections might help to determine an approximate optimal level, but rarely is an election about one particular issue alone
- o These are some goods that government often provides; are they "public"?
  - police & fire protection[46]
  - roads

---

[46] Dorchester County, SC, adopted an ordinance with a fee schedule for rescue operations involving non-residents. The ordinance was passed in July 2015, and is available here: https://www2.municode.com/library/sc/dorchester%20county/codes/code_of_ordinances. The fee schedule is not attached, but a draft showed an hourly charge of $305 for "heavy apparatus" including fire engines, as well as "extrication with the use of hydraulic tools and landing zone" for $2,335. These fees are apparently charger after-the-fact. In contrast, see an interesting example of fire protection provided to non-residents of a Tennessee county, only if an annual fee is paid in advance: https://www.youtube.com/watch?v=PwJrPa8Ps7A.

- health care
- education
- national defense
- water & electricity
- fireworks displays
  - If the above examples are not "public goods," does this mean government should not provide them?
    - that is a separate issue, one on which reasonable people can disagree
    - the point is that private markets *could* provide them efficiently if they're not purely public

- **Optimal Quantity of Public Goods**
  - We can provide a theoretical explanation for the optimal quantity of public goods provision by government
  - However, it would be extremely difficult to achieve this optimal amount in reality.

LECTURE L: THE U.S. TAX SYSTEM & ALTERNATIVES

The U.S. federal income tax system is an absolute mess. In fact, compliance and enforcement can employ an entire (socially wasteful) profession. The tax code is filled with arbitrary and ever-changing rules and regulations, incomprehensible to taxpayers and the politicians who write the rules.

In 2009 President Obama vowed to reform the tax code. Nothing substantive happened during his 8 years. President Trump vowed to reform the tax code, and the Tax Cuts and Jobs Act of 2017 was enacted on December 22. The Act reduces marginal tax rates for most taxpayers. Usually, promises for significant tax reform are laughable. But the tax cuts for 2018 were perhaps Trump's most important accomplishment so far.

It is interesting to note that sometimes Presidents' staff members cannot or do not follow tax law. Of course, President Trump hasn't released his own tax returns, so we have no idea how well he's followed the rules. In February 2017, Trump appointed Rep. Mick Mulvaney (R-SC) as Director of the Office of Management and Budget, despite his admitting to failing to pay taxes related to a "household employee."[47] Will you be surprised if other examples arise? Several members of Obama's Cabinet admitted to cheating (well, "making mistakes") on their taxes. Tim Geithner who as Treasury Secretary (2009-13) oversaw the IRS is one example.[48] Tom Daschle and other Cabinet appointees withdrew their nominations because of potential "tax problems." Of course, many other examples could probably be cited; these are just those cases that received a lot of publicity.

Politicians gain power by manipulating the tax code, and they are not likely to give up this power by simplifying the system in any significant or permanent way. But there are some good alternatives to our current income tax system.

---

[47] https://www.washingtonpost.com/news/powerpost/wp/2017/01/18/trump-budget-nominee-failed-to-pay-15000-in-taxes-related-to-household-employee/?utm_term=.6bcb5ea4bade

[48] http://abcnews.go.com/Business/story?id=6704526

- **The Federal Income Tax**
  - Here we show the tax tables for <u>single taxpayers</u>.
    - it's different for married couples
  - Our focus is on marginal tax rates – the rate of tax on the next dollar you earn
    - the marginal tax rates apply to "taxable income," which is gross income minus exemptions and deductions
  - Changes resulting from the Tax Cuts and Jobs Act of 2017 are illustrated in Table L.1

Table L.1. Comparison of key tax law variables, 2017-18, individual taxpayer

	2017	2018
Standard deduction	$6,350	$12,000
Exemptions (each)	$4,050	n/a
Child tax credit (each)*	$1,000	$2,000
Highest marginal tax rate	39.6%	37%

* The child tax credit phases out with income. For 2017, the credit is reduced $50 per $1,000 income over $75,000. In 2018, the phaseout begins with income over $200,000 (http://turbotax.intuit.com/).

  - See Tables L.2 and L.3 for what the federal income tax brackets looked like in 2001 and 2017

Table L.2. Federal income tax table, individual taxpayer, 2001

Taxable Income	Marginal Tax Rate
$0 – 27,050	15%
$27,051 – 65,550	27.5%
$65,551 – 136,750	30.5%
$136,751 – 297,350	35.5%
$297,351 and above	39.1%

Table L.3. Federal income tax table, individual taxpayer, 2017

Taxable Income	Marginal Tax Rate	Tax Amount (rounded to the nearest $)
$0 – 9,325	10%	10% of taxable income
$9,326 – 37,950	15%	$932.50 + 15% of amt. over $9,325
$37,951 – 91,900	25%	$5,226 + 25% of amt. over $37,950
$91,901 – 191,650	28%	$18,714 + 28% of amt. over $91,900
$191,651 – 416,700	33%	$46,644 + 33% of amt. over $191,650
$416,701 – 418,400	35%	$120,910 + 35% of amt. over $416,700
$418,401 and above	39.6%	$121,505 + 39.6% of amt. over $418,400

Source: https://taxfoundation.org/2017-tax-brackets/

- o Calculating your income tax is not simple...
  - ■ Ex: let's calculate the tax burden for a person with taxable income of $80,000 in 2001
    - • suppose income goes up at the same rate as inflation (38% over the time period), so that income in 2017 is $110,570

Your tax in 2001 is calculated:
= ($27,050 x 0.15) + ([$65,550-27,050] x 0.275) + ([80,000-65,550) x 0.305
= 4057.50 + 10,587.50 + 4,407.25 = **$19,052.25**
Average tax rate is tax paid/taxable income, or 23.8%

Your tax in 2017 is calculated:
= $18,714 + ([110,570-91,900] x 0.28)
= $18,714 + $4,667.50 = **$23,381.50**
Average tax rate is 21.3%

  - ■ The average tax rate decreased from 23.8% to 21.3% for this worker
    - • so the tax regressivity has decreased
  - o Now let's see what happens for the same person in 2018
    - ■ Accounting for inflation, the same person's income would be $113,840 in 2018
    - ■ the 2018 tax table is shown in Table L.4
      - • Trump had wanted just 3 brackets (12%, 25%, 33%), but couldn't make it happen

Table L.4. Federal income tax table,
individual taxpayer, 2018

Taxable Income	Marginal Tax Rate
$0 – 9,525	10%
$9,526 – 38.700	12%
$38,701 – 82,500	22%
$82,501 – 157,500	24%
$157,501 – 200,000	32%
$200,001 – 500,000	35%
over $500,000	37%

Your tax in 2018 is calculated using income in these brackets:
10%, 12%, 22%, and 24%:

$$= \$952.50 + \$3,501 + \$9,636 + 7,521.60$$
$$= \mathbf{\$21,611.10}$$

Average tax rate is 19.0%

- **Debate over Corporate Tax Cuts in 2017**
  - For 2018 the corporate tax rate decreases from a 35% top rate (graduated) to a flat 21%
    - the corporate tax rate cut is permanent
  - The personal income tax cuts (illustrated in 2018 vs 2017 tax tables, above) are set to expire in 2025
    - this was one of the main criticisms of the bill in media coverage
    - from CNN: "But here's the thing: After 2025, all individual tax cuts are set to expire. At the same time, corporate rate cuts are made permanent under the bill."
  - Astonishing example of incompetent media reporting
    - during the debate in late 2017, I never saw *anyone* consider the fact that in 2024 or 2025, the story will be "individual tax rates are set to increase in 2025, unless Congress and the President act to keep tax rate cuts in place"
      - there would be enormous political pressure for them to act to keep the cuts in place

- in this sense, this compromise was a very good political move for proponents of the 2017 Act
  - Trump and the republicans deserve credit for making this happen, politically
    - disclaimer: I like the plan because I'll have a lower tax rate, and much higher child tax credit
  - In July 2018, some members of the House of Reps began efforts to make the individual tax cuts permanent after 2025[49]
  - Given that most people will be seeing higher take-home pay, I'd expect the Act to be more popular than the media expects

- **State Taxes**
  - State governments get their revenue from property taxes, sales taxes, and, in most states, income taxes
    - 37% of state tax collections (U.S. overall)
  - Table L.5 shows state income taxes, lowest rate and highest rate, for 2018
    - South Carolina, and several other states, have very low incomes for their highest tax bracket threshold
      - might as well call it a 7% flat tax...
    - some states tax only dividend and interest income (i.e., from investments)
  - When you add federal and state income taxes, sales taxes, property taxes, etc., you may very well pay ¼ to ½ of your overall income in taxes
    - consider your situation in Charleston: 20% federal income tax, 6% state income tax, 9% sales tax, various excise taxes, property taxes, etc.

---

[49] https://www.washingtonpost.com/business/house-gop-launches-push-for-permanent-individual-tax-cuts/2018/07/24/f6ed7e62-8f6b-11e8-ae59-01880eac5f1d_story.html?noredirect=on&utm_term=.e3e76af07ef1

Table L.5. State income tax rate ranges (2018)

State	Low rate (%)	High rate (%)	State	Low Rate (%)	High rate (%)
Alabama	2.0	5.0	Nebraska	2.46	6.84
Alaska	none	--	Nevada	none	--
Arizona	2.59	4.54	N. Hampshire	5% (div/int inc)	
Arkansas	0.9	6.9	New Jersey	1.4	8.97
California	1.0	13.3	New Mexico	1.7	4.9
Colorado	4.63	(flat)	New York	4.0	8.82
Connecticut	3.0	6.99	N. Carolina	5.5	(flat)
Delaware	2.2	6.6	North Dakota	1.10	2.90
Florida	none	--	Ohio	1.98	5.0
Georgia	1.0	6.0	Oklahoma	0.5	5.0
Hawaii	1.4	11.0	Oregon	5.0	9.9
Idaho	1.6	7.4	Pennsylvania	3.07	(flat)
Illinois	4.95	(flat)	Rhode Island	3.75	5.99
Indiana	3.23	(flat)	**S. Carolina**	**3.0**	**7.0***
Iowa	0.36	8.98	South Dakota	none	--
Kansas	3.1	5.7	Tennessee	3% (div/int inc)	
Kentucky	2.0	6.0	Texas	none	--
Louisiana	2.0	6.0	Utah	5.0	(flat)
Maine	5.8	7.15	Vermont	3.55	8.95
Maryland	2.0	5.75	Virginia	2.0	5.75
Massachusetts	5.10	(flat)	Washington	none	--
Michigan	4.25	(flat)	West Virginia	3.0	6.5
Minnesota	5.35	9.85	Wisconsin	4.0	7.65
Mississippi	3.0	5.0	Wyoming	none	--
Missouri	1.5	5.9	D. C.	4.0	8.95
Montana	1.0	6.9			

* The highest rate of 7% in SC is applied to taxable income above $14,860. States vary in their income brackets, standard deductions, etc.

Source: https://taxfoundation.org/state-individual-income-tax-rates-brackets-2018/

- **Income Taxes and Incentives**
  - Income taxes will potentially affect incentives, as Laffer noted
    - the Laffer curve shows tax revenue as a function of tax rate (Figure L.1)
    - Laffer was a motivating force behind Reagan cutting MTRs in the early 1980s

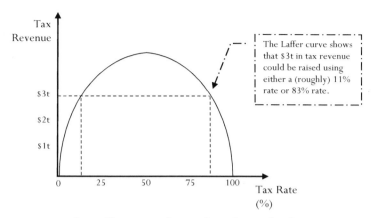

Figure L.1. The Laffer curve shows the relationship between tax rate and tax revenue, through the tax disincentive to work

- the major problem with Reagan's economic policies in the 1980s weren't on the tax side, it was the inability to cut government spending
- this idea has been coined "trickle-down" or supply-side economics
- it is legitimate in theory, but politicians have put a spin on it
  - Do higher taxes make you want to work less?
    - the highest MTR in the early 1960s was 92%

- **What's "Fair"?**
  - People disagree on what's fair
    - the Occupy Wall Street protest group was upset about the top 1% of income earners
      - slogan "we are the 99%"
    - others might argue that everyone should pay the same tax rate
  - Do the "rich" pay their "fair share" of federal income taxes?

- the top 0.1% (160,000 families) hold 22% of America's wealth[50]
- at the other end, NTU suggests that 34% of 2015 *tax returns* paid $0 income tax
  o Consider the amount of the federal personal income tax revenue paid by income class (Table L.6)
    - are the top 1% paying enough?
    - of course, that's normative

Table L.6. Who paid what percentage of federal income taxes in 2015?

Percentiles, ranked by AGI	AGI threshold on percentiles	Adjusted Gross Income Share	% of federal personal inc. taxes paid
Top 1%	$480,930	20.7%	39%
Top 5%	$195,778	36.1%	60%
Top 10%	$138,031	47.4%	71%
Top 25%	$79,655	69.0%	87%
Top 50%	$39,275	88.7%	97%
Bottom 50%	<$39,275	11.3%	3%

Note: AGI is Adjusted Gross Income
Source: National Taxpayers Union, https://www.ntu.org/foundation/tax-page/who-pays-income-taxes

- **Tax Politics**
  o How likely are we to see higher "taxes on the rich"?
    - half the population doesn't pay taxes – what are they likely to vote for?
    - are reductions in government (deficit) spending likely, when half the people don't pay taxes?
  o We have a "progressive" tax rate structure
    - this means the average tax rate (ATR) increases as income rises
      • but if marginal tax rates (MTR) increase as income increases, so must ATR

---

[50] http://www.economist.com/news/finance-and-economics/21631129-it-001-who-are-really-getting-ahead-america-forget-1

- A "regressive" tax would be one where the average tax rate increases as income *falls* – most people think that would not be fair
- "Vertical equity" and "horizontal equity" are important principles in tax theory, most economists agree on these
  - vertical equity: people with higher incomes should pay a higher percentage in taxes
  - horizontal equity: people with the same incomes should pay the same in taxes

- **Compliance Costs**
  - One of the major problems with the current system is "compliance costs" or "excess burden"
    - recently estimated at $262 billion[51]
      - value of 7 billion hours of time, worth about $229 billion at average wage rate
      - $34 billion in software & tax services
    - about 8% of total government revenues ($3.316 trillion in 2017)
  - Some groups have a strong incentive in keeping the tax system complicated
    - tax accountants and lawyers
    - Intuit, the creator of Turbo Tax software, spent $11.5 million over 5 years, lobbying Congress to keep the federal system complicated[52]
    - yet the IRS apparently favors simplification[53]
  - Consider alternative forms of taxation
    - Fair Tax (national sales tax) is becoming more popular[54]

---

[51] https://www.ntu.org/foundation/detail/tax-complexity-2017

[52] http://abcnews.go.com/Business/turbotax-lobbies-lawmakers-tax-code-complicated/story?id=18882377

[53] https://fairtax.org/articles/irs-boss-koskinen-backs-tax-reform-calls-system-a-mess

[54] See http://fairtax.org/ for information.

- I like this idea a lot
  - flat-rate income tax
    - but what is the definition of "income" or "taxable income" – that can be manipulated by politicians
  - a major benefit of changing the income tax is a decrease in "excess burden" or tax collection costs
  - a major change should also tie politicians' hands and make it more difficult for them to give out political favors to their friends and campaign contributors

- **Final Thoughts on Public Finance**
  - o Can we sustain current spending levels?
  - o Will voters ever get serious and demand spending cuts?

LECTURE M: POLITICAL ECONOMY/OTHER TOPICS

If we have extra time, we can cover some more current events and policy issues. I will provide handouts in class, or webpage material, as needed.

End-of-semester note:

Hopefully you feel like you have developed some useful tools in this class. I hope that you are able to better analyze current economic events, government policies, and politicians' rhetoric.

The next course in the economics sequence is ECON 201, Principles of Macroeconomics. Even if you are not required to take it, I would highly recommend it. That class gives a good foundation of what most people think of when they hear "economics." It basically covers "the economy" – inflation, economic growth, interest rates, recessions, etc.

I hope you enjoyed this course!

Study Aids – Introduction

The remainder of this book contains study aids that you may use to help you learn the material for the course. None of this is required or graded. However, I strongly recommend you work through these materials as we go through the course.

The problem sets include a variety of questions. Some relate to very specific issues we discuss in the lectures; others are more general or abstract. They are not intended to just give you a preview of exam questions. However, if you can answer these questions, I would expect that you will do well on the exams. The "brief solutions" provided are not necessarily the only responses to the questions, so ask if you have any questions about these. Questions denoted with "(H)" come from or are adapted from Paul Heyne's excellent book, *The Economic Way of Thinking*, 9e (1999). Other questions are original, and some are based on current or recent events.

The example test questions can be helpful in preparing for exams, but I do not recommend that you try to memorize these. Instead, you should focus on *understanding* the material. I will expect you to apply the material we cover, not simply repeat it or define vocabulary words. The answers are provided at the end of each section. You should try to work through the questions prior to checking answers.

Feel free to ask if you have any questions at all about these materials.

PROBLEM SETS AND RECOMMENDED SOLUTIONS

Lecture A: Overview of Economics

1. Prior to the increase in the highway speed limit in the 1980s, it was common to hear the saying, "Drive 55, Save Lives." If this is a legitimate policy to follow, why not eliminate driving all together and save even more lives? What about this rule: "Drive 125, Save Time"? Is this legitimate? How should we deal with the conflicting goals of safety and saving time? If we're serious about travel safety, then why do we allow airplane travel?

2. In his article, "More Sex is Safer Sex...," Landsburg argues that "sexually conservative" individuals would help to slow the rate of the spread of AIDS if they became "less conservative." Would you expect politicians, religious leaders, parents, etc., to endorse such an argument? Why not? Does this mean that his argument is invalid?

3. In *The Armchair Economist*, Landsburg argues that we could decrease the number of auto fatalities by replacing seatbelts, airbags, etc., with a spear mounted in the steering column aimed at the driver's heart. How could this possibly reduce the number of auto fatalities?

4. Explain why models – which are admittedly unrealistic – are useful tools for analyzing behavior. (Recall the roadmap example.)

5. Distinguish between "selfish" behavior and "self-interested" behavior. Is giving money to a church selfish behavior? Is it self-interested behavior?

6. A newspaper story reported that two-thirds of all mothers who work outside the home "do it for the money, not by choice." Are those really alternatives? Either for the money or by choice? (*H*)

7. Are the following statements positive or normative? (a) Taxes should be raised on the wealthiest citizens. (b) The wealthiest 0.1% of Americans own 22% of U.S. wealth. (c) Jose Cuervo tequila tastes disgusting. (d) Government programs should not discourage hard work. (e) The U.S. unemployment rate

is 11.5%. (f) Economics is a tough course. (g) The "Cash for Clunkers" program is stupid. (h) The financial and auto sector bailouts ended up costing us more than $2 trillion.

8. Let's suppose you bought a $10 ticket to Mel and the Party Hats' last concert ever. Unfortunately, the night of the show, you fall ill and cannot go out on the town. If tickets cannot be returned, and you want to sell yours, what is the minimum price you should accept?

9. At the College of Charleston, an assistant professor of English might get a 9-month salary of $60,000, while an assistant professor of accounting could get over $140,000. What economic concept explains such a large difference in salary for two professors of different disciplines?

10. Describe the full cost of going to eat at FIG at 7:00 on a Friday evening. Does "cost" only include menu prices? How might the use of www.opentable.com affect your cost?

11. Suppose U.S. commercial airlines will carry an infant under the age of two at no charge if the infant sits on the lap of a fare-paying adult, but will charge for an extra seat if the plane is full and the parents want the child placed in a child-restraint seat. If the government requires that all infants fly in child-restraint seats, the infant will have to have a ticket of its own to make sure that a seat is available. Should the government impose such a requirement? "There is no real choice in the matter," some have argued, "because a child's life is of far more value than the price of an airline ticket." Do you agree with that argument? What are the actual alternatives? (H)

12. There is an important difference between correlation and causality, yet this is often ignored by politicians, reporters, and voters. Consider the following three cases. (H)

    a. Carl bought four steaks at Publix Friday morning. Later, Shake, Frylock, and Meatwad came over for a barbecue. Do you suppose Carl's purchase of the steaks *caused* the friends to come over? How can you decide which event was more likely the cause and which the effect?

    b. If you read that the crime rate increased in a certain city during a time when the purchase of handguns had also increased, would you suspect a causal connection? Which would more likely be the cause and which the effect? How does *theory* shape your answer?

13. Your boss tells you in an angry voice, "I don't care what you learned in economics. If you don't include all our sunk costs in your report and recommendation, I'll fire you." Are the sunk costs now irrelevant to your decision making? (*H*)

Brief Solutions to Problem Set A

1. Safety isn't the only thing we value; we also value our time. There's a trade-off between getting places quicker and safety.

2. Most "leaders" probably would not endorse this because it's not exactly how you'd probably raise kids. In any case, just because it's not popular doesn't mean it's an invalid argument.

3. The spear would be a strong incentive to drive more safely, so there would be fewer accidents. (Of course each accident that does occur would result in certain death.)

4. They ignore irrelevant details, making the world easier to analyze.

5. Selfish behavior generally means you're trying to help yourself, maybe to the detriment of others. Self-interested behavior is to the benefit of the actor, and may help others.

6. It's a choice. You can have a low standard of living, or you can work for a better one.

7. a. normative, b. positive, c. normative, d. normative, e. positive, f. normative, g. normative, h. positive

8. The highest positive price you can get.

9. Opportunity cost: an accounting Ph.D. has numerous career alternatives in the private sector; an English Ph.D. maybe doesn't so much.

10. The $, plus the time parking, waiting for a table, and eating. There may be other costs too. The use of "Open Table" can lower the time costs if it reduces your wait for a table.

11. The law requiring infants to have a seat might cause more kids' deaths. The parents would have to pay for an extra seat on the plane, so it'll be more expensive to fly. They're more likely to just drive, which is much more dangerous than

flying. (The number of deaths in 1 month from driving is equal to about 40 years of deaths from airline travel.)

12. a. The two events are probably related, but probably not through a causal relationship. Theory: you need to have some idea about how the world works. Be careful of the *post hoc ergo propter hoc* logical fallacy. b. There may be a causal connection, but it could run either way.

13. Now the sunk cost is relevant because it will affect your job in the future.

Lecture B: Specialization and Trade

14. According to the principle of comparative advantage, specialization and trade increases the world's total output (production) and consumption. Explain why.

For questions 15-19, consider the countries Russia (R) and Switzerland (S), which produce only vodka and wristwatches, according to the PPFs listed in the tables below. Each column represents one point on the PPF. For example, Russia can produce 100 cases vodka only if it produces zero watches.

Russia—Production Possibilities			
Vodka	100	50	0
Watches	0	50	100

Switzerland—Production Possibilities			
Vodka	60	30	0
Watches	0	10	20

15. Draw the PPFs for both countries. Be sure to label the axes.
16. Which country has the absolute advantage in the production of vodka? In watches?
17. In terms of watches, what is S's opportunity cost of producing 1 unit of vodka?
18. Which country has the comparative advantage in the production of vodka? Of watches?
19. What is the range of exchange prices at which both countries might potentially agree? (a) Put the answer in terms of watches per case of vodka. (b) Now answer in terms of cases of vodka per watch.
20. If economics suggests that trade is so beneficial, then why do you think so many politicians and special interest groups (e.g., labor unions, the textile, auto, and steel industries in the U.S.) support government policies like import tariffs, and other restrictions on imported goods?

21. Why is it that trade — whether or not it is allowed to occur — is unlikely to have much of an effect on the overall level of employment in a particular country?

Brief Solutions to Problem Set B

14. When producers specialize, they get better at producing. So everyone specializes in what they're good at, so total production goes up.
15. (You should be able to draw this.)
16. V: R has the absolute advantage; W: R has the absolute advantage
17. S's opportunity cost of producing $1V = 1/3W$
18. V: S has comparative advantage; R has comparative advantage in W.
19. In R: 1V costs 1W and 1W costs 1V; in S: $1V = 1/3W$ and $1W = 3V$. So... (a) 1V will trade for between 1/3 and 1W; (b) 1W will trade for between 1 and 3V
20. Because these people expect benefits at the expense of others. Politicians get votes and campaign contributions, and lobbying industries get monetary benefits for themselves.
21. Because specialization & trade basically just affects the <u>allocation</u> of jobs among industries, not the overall level of employment.

Lectures C, D, and E: Supply, Demand, Markets & Prices
[I recommend completing these after we have gone through all
three sections, C, D, and E.]

22. The late Sen. Ted Kennedy proclaimed that health care
    should be "a fundamental right of everyone, not a privilege."
    But the assertion of rights logically entails the assertion of
    obligations. Your right to vote, for example, entails the
    obligation of election officials to accept and count your ballot;
    your right to use your own umbrella implies an obligation on
    the part of others not to borrow it without your permission.
    (*H*)
    a. In 1967 the president of the American Medical
       Association was quoted as saying that medical care was a
       privilege and not a right. Today the AMA officially
       proclaims, "health care is the right of everyone." Why do
       you think they changed their opinion? What quantity and
       quality of health care do you suppose the AMA is talking
       about? Is a liver transplant, for example, the right of
       everyone with a diseased liver?
    b. If "health care is the right of everyone," who has the
       obligation to provide health care to everyone?
    c. A report released by the National Center for Health
       Services Research states that use of primary care services
       at a leading health maintenance organization fell 11%
       when the HMO imposed a $5 charge per office visit.
       What does this suggest about the "need" for health care?
23. The Bill of Rights, the first ten amendments to the
    Constitution of the United States, says nothing about a right
    to housing. Some have nonetheless argued that housing is a
    more fundamental and important right than the rights now
    protected by the first amendment (freedom of religion, of
    speech, of the press, and of political assembly). Would you
    be in favor of adding a right to housing to the Bill of Rights?
    Defend your answer. (*H*)
24. Not long ago, the acres of grass surrounding the Taj Mahal in
    Agra, India, are cut by young women who slice off handfuls
    with short kitchen blades. Is this a low- or high-cost way to

keep the law mowed? Why don't people in the U.S. use this method? (*H*)

25. Hurricane Katrina caused enormous damage, and caused a huge increase in the demand for carpenters' services. If carpenters respond by raising their hourly rates, the cost to property owners of having their buildings repaired or rebuilt will rise. But does a hurricane raise the **cost** *to carpenters* of repairing buildings? Or are carpenters who raise their rates merely taking unfair advantage of the situation? Hint: Keep in mind that "cost" in economics means "opportunity cost." (*H*)

26. Why do parking lot fees vary so widely from city to city in the United States? Annual parking at a small town college in Georgia costs $80 per year, while parking in a garage in downtown Charleston costs $700 per year. Does this difference reflect the greater greed of Charleston property owners? (*H*)

27. Explain the following statement by a military recruiter: "There's nothing like a good recession to cure our recruiting problems." (*H*)

28. Many parts of the country saw record breaking droughts in the summer of 2007, and some experts were predicting the largest jump in the U.S. crop acreage since World War II. What would prompt farmers to undertake such a public-spirited response to the situation created by the drought? (*H*)

29. Is smallpox virus rare today? Is it scarce? What's the difference? (*H*)

30. There are no toll charges for crossing bridges from downtown to West Ashley or Mt. Pleasant during rush hour. How is the scarce space on the bridges rationed? (*H*)

31. A parking space in the 1500-car garage under the Boston Common cost $110 a month in 1988, according to an article in *The New York Times*. Those who want to rent a space could expect a seven-year wait, according to the state agency that runs the garage. Is the rate too high, too low, or about right, in your judgment? What do you think would happen to the monthly parking rate if the garage were privately owned? Why doesn't the state raise the rate? (*H*)

32. If the supply of turkeys in a particular November turned out to be unusually small, do you think a turkey shortage would result? Why or why not? What about pumpkins in October or roses in February? (*H*)

33. Renters in Honolulu must pay three times as much and renters in Chicago two times as much for an apartment as renters in Colorado Springs. Charleston rentals are also expensive! Is that fair? Why does it occur? Should the government offer subsidies to Honolulu and Chicago renters? What would happen? (*H*)

34. Do students put more effort into courses when they have to pay higher tuition to take the courses? (*H*)

35. Obviously governments can have a large influence on the functions of markets. Does a government have the ability to eliminate markets, say by making them illegal? (In other words, is a law that makes certain transactions likely to eliminate those transactions? Can you cite some examples?) Can you predict any of the effects of such laws?

36. Should the casualties already incurred in a war be taken into account by a government in deciding whether it is in the national interest to continue the war? This is obviously not a trivial question. You can hear Iraq death tolls reported daily on the news. This is a much more difficult question than you might at first suppose, especially for politicians depending on popular support. (*H*)

37. The deputy chairman of the Russian Red Cross complained in the 1990s that food aid sent to the country by Western nations was being stolen. "Russian swindlers are the most experienced in the world," he said. The deputy director of the Russian aid commission expressed the need for a centralized system to ensure proper distribution. Which do you think is likely to get into the mouths of hungry people faster and with less loss through spoilage: food that is distributed through government agencies and charity organizations or food that has been stolen? Why? (*H*)

38. If the desire for money is an indication of a selfish and materialistic attitude, as many people seem to think, why do

churches and charitable organizations work so hard to acquire more of it? (*H*)

39. Some people believe that the recently high gas prices are an argument for having the government ration gasoline by the criterion of *need*. How would you propose that the rationing authorities determine "need"? How does the price system compare to the alternatives. (*H*)

40. Suppose that you own and operate a grocery store. As you're preparing to go to work in the morning, you hear on the radio that the price of peanut butter has been raised by the processors because of a large increase in the price of peanuts. You remember that just yesterday you received a new shipment of peanut butter – a two-month supply in fact – and you are rejoicing in the knowledge that you won't have to raise your price for two months. Then the phone rings. Prof. Walker is on the line, and he knows about your peanut butter situation and tries to persuade you that it is your *social duty* to raise the price of your peanut butter as soon as you get to the store. What argument would he use, and why would he be correct? (*H*)

41. Explain the difference between a *change in quantity demanded* (ΔQ_d) and a *change in demand* (ΔD).

42. Explain the relationship between the law of decreasing marginal utility and the demand curve.

43. Explain in detail how the market equilibrium price and quantity adjusts after there is a change in supply or demand.

44. South Carolina shrimpers say that shrimp prices were higher before the BP gulf oil spill in 2010, and lower after the spill. As a result of the oil spill, did the S or D of shrimp move more? (Answer this given that Q shrimp fell after the spill.)

Figures (a) – (h), below, depict changes in demand and supply. Draw a graph to illustrate each situation described in questions 45-57. Then check to make sure you graphs look similar to those below. Be sure that you can explain why each curve shifts the way it does. Explain how equilibrium price and quantity change as a result of the change(s) listed in each situation.

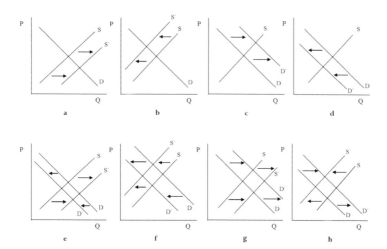

45. In the market for luxury cars: the effect of an increase in consumers' current income.
46. In the market for wheat: a report is released showing that wheat bread prevents cancer; farmers experience favorable weather this year.
47. In the market for cocaine: more police are hired to arrest dealers; many drug users overdose and die.
48. In the market for hot dogs (an inferior good): the effect of an increase in consumers' expected future incomes.
49. In the market for coffee: the effect of a decrease in the price of tea (a substitute for coffee).
50. In the market for marijuana: word spreads that marijuana actually isn't that harmful.
51. In the market for college education: factory wage rates increase substantially.
52. In the market for cassette tapes: the price of plastic falls; cars are no longer equipped with tape players.
53. In the market for Spam: people's current income drops; road-kill animals (whose meat is used in Spam) becomes less common.

54. In the market for snow skis: the snowfall this season is higher than expected; workers in Austria (a major ski-producing country) become more productive.
55. In the market for gasoline: both consumers and producers expect future prices to be much higher.
56. In the market for gasoline: the effect of a decrease in the price of crude oil, an input to gas.
57. In the market for water skis: ski-factory workers go on strike.

Brief Solutions to Problem Set C, D, and E

22. (a) Difficult question. But the reason the AMA changed its perspective is probably that now government wants to "provide" health care, and the public seems to agree. So why not advocate it if government will pay for it? (b) Good question. Why should I have to pay for your health care? Why not everyone pay for himself? (c) It's not a need.
23. Hopefully your answer is "no." If you say "yes," then who should be responsible to provide the housing?
24. Low cost – labor is plentiful and cheap in India, compared to capital.
25. Yes, the hurricane raises the cost to the carpenters. The opportunity cost of taking the day off, for example, increases significantly after a hurricane. If you don't think about it, you might just react that this is taking advantage of the situation.
26. The opportunity cost of land varies across cities.
27. During a recession, some people lose their jobs, and the unemployed have a more difficult time finding jobs. With fewer alternatives, more people consider going into the military.
28. The drought probably caused S to fall, so P rose. As a result, it was more profitable for people to devote their land to farming. It wasn't due to "public spirit," but rather a response to a profit incentive.
29. Smallpox is rare, but not scarce. For something to be scarce, it has to be wanted, not just rare.
30. First-come-first-served.

31. The money price is too low; that's why there's a waiting list. If it was privately owned, the price would certainly be higher. The government doesn't really care about raising revenues efficiently or about people on waiting lists.
32. No, a shortage would not result unless the price was restricted. Price adjusts to equate S and D.
33. I don't know whether it's fair, but it's the result of relative scarcity, of which the price is a signal. If people don't want to pay high rent, they can move somewhere else less expensive. If you subsidize people to live in certain places, more people will want to live there, making the original problem even worse.
34. I would expect students to put more effort into a course if they have to pay for it (say, compared to having a lottery scholarship). If price just goes up a bit I don't think effort would go up too much.
35. No, government can't eliminate markets simply by making them illegal. The illegal drug market is a good example. Once illegal, people just get the goods on the black market.
36. According to the sunk cost argument, no. However, if the number of lives already lost will affect the number of lives to be lost in the future, then the information is relevant. Obviously this is a tough call for any politician.
37. The thieves are probably more efficient at getting the food to the hungry. They're interested in selling it quickly; the government employees have no personal stake in ensuring the food doesn't spoil.
38. Money is "liquid." It can be easily converted to whatever's needed.
39. Good question. If you think about this, it would be very difficult to come up with a way of allocating the gas.
40. The argument is that the opportunity cost of replacing your peanut butter inventory has increased, so you should raise the price. The higher price will signal to consumers that peanut butter has become scarcer, and they may wish to consider alternatives. The higher price will allocate the peanut butter to those who value it most.
41. Review your lecture notes if you can't answer this!

42. Since people get less and less satisfaction from each additional unit consumed, they'd be willing to pay less for each subsequent unit. That's why the demand curve has a negative slope.
43. Again, review your notes to answer this.
44. If the equilibrium P and Q *after* the spill were both lower than before, it means the new intersection between S and D has to be "southwest" of the original equilibrium. This means that demand must have fallen more than supply.
45. For 45-57, I suggest you draw a graph first, then find the correct match among options a-h. (c is the correct graph to illustrate 45.)
46. g
47. f
48. d
49. d
50. c
51. d
52. e
53. h
54. g
55. h
56. a
57. b

Lecture F: Markets and Economic Efficiency

58. On July 27, 2007, Nike and Reebok announced that they were suspending all clothing sales with Michael Vick's name or number. This action followed the charges filed surrounding Vick's role in dog fights, torture, and executions. Why did they need to announce that they would no longer sell shoes and t-shirts? Do you think anyone was still buying them anyway?

59. Consider the concepts of consumer's and producer's surplus. Why do you think some people view market economies as "evil" since sellers apparently earn profit at the expense of consumers? Aren't the consumers benefiting from transactions too? Explain.

60. In economics, transactions are assumed to be acts of voluntary self-interested behavior. Therefore, the maximization of voluntary transactions tends to increase the overall happiness in society, since with each transaction, at least two people are better off and no one is worse off.
    a. Explain the price (in any particular market) at which overall happiness is maximized.
    b. Explain the statement, "At the market equilibrium price, no one in the market is unsatisfied."
    c. Is there any other price, other than Pe, for which the statement in (b) is true?
    d. What does the imposition of a price control law do to overall welfare and economic efficiency?
       (i). What does a price ceiling do to the quantity of transactions and the social surplus?
       (ii). What does a price floor do to the quantity of transactions and the social surplus?

61. Can you explain why the quantity of voluntary, mutually beneficial transactions is maximized at the equilibrium price?
    a. Why do politicians advocate price controls that *must* reduce the quantity of socially beneficial transactions?
    b. Why don't the wise citizens of the U.S. protest economically inefficient policies? Are citizens irrational?

    c.   Do you think government knows better how to allocate resources than the market system? Explain.

62. "The market price mechanism ensures that the production of each good or service comes from the most efficient producer(s). Once the goods & services are produced, the price mechanism ensures that they are consumed by the consumers with the greatest demand for the products." Make sure you thoroughly understand this.

63. Why is it important that prices in a market economy be allowed to change in response to changing demand and supply conditions? What functions do these changing prices perform?

64. One reason that local governments sometimes impose rent controls is precisely to prevent money prices from rationing scarce residential space. Do the controls succeed in doing this? How has it happened, do you suppose, that most of New York City's rent-controlled apartments are occupied by relatively wealthy people? (*H*)

65. In late April 2011, ABC News reported that the top 5 oil companies (BP, ConocoPhillips, Exxon/Mobil, Chevron, and Shell) earned $35 billion in profit during the first quarter of 2011, and yet gas prices are at record highs for the month of April. Is this a demonstration that profit is money "taken from consumers"? Does this prove that "profit is evil"?

Brief Solutions to Problem Set F

58. I doubt anyone was buying the products anymore anyway. They probably made these announcements for publicity.

59. Consumers are getting CS, analogous to the profit (PS) that producers get. Firms have to report profit and pay taxes on it. Consumers don't have to report or pay taxes on CS. Maybe this partially explains why people seem to ignore the mutually beneficial aspect of market transactions.

60. (a) the equilibrium price; (b) At Pe, everyone who wants to engage in a transaction (either buyer or seller) can find someone to transact with, since Qd=Qs; (c) no; (d) lowers

them; (i) reduces the number of transactions, and reduces (CS+PS); (ii) same answer as (i). You can draw a picture to help answer this one.

61. (a) Price controls are popular, probably because no one knows anything about economics. (b) Typically the costs of arguing against stupid policies aren't worth it, while the policy beneficiaries lobby hard to get their concentrated benefits; (c) If you understand the stuff in this class, you should say the market is more efficient in allocation.

62. No comment required.

63. Prices need to adjust to ensure that scarce resources are allocated efficiently. Profitable firms will be able to continue production; the lowest-cost manufacturers will stay in business. On the demand side, those with more $ will be able to buy more. This is a brief answer, but make sure you understand this thoroughly.

64. Rent controls cause a number of unintended consequences, as discussed in class. Rich people can still get into the apartments by paying "key deposits," or otherwise getting favor with those offering the apartments.

65. It's very odd to think of "profit" as money "taken from consumers." After all, these are voluntary transactions. "Profit is evil" is a very extreme statement that reflects a poor understanding of markets.

158

Lecture G: Government Price Controls

66. If you do not want free markets and prices to ration scarce goods and services, how should they be allocated?
67. Explain the unintended consequences of price controls like rent controls, minimum wage laws, and agriculture price supports.
68. Would you support price ceilings on medical care? How would you overcome the shortages that would result?
69. Draw a graph to illustrate a price floor on corn production. What is the likely result of this policy? Who benefits and who is harmed? Is this a policy we should have in the U.S.?
70. *The Post and Courier* (7/12/07) published an article which reported the results of a study which show that the gap between what whites and blacks pay for mortgages is greater in Charleston than in any other major city in the country. John Edwards mentioned this article in the democratic debates that were held at The Citadel the next week. Is racial discrimination the cause for this disparity? Or is there likely a better explanation? Should the government mandate that all people should pay the same mortgage rates? How should credit histories play into the way mortgages are priced?
71. Draw a graph that illustrates an effective (or binding) rent control law in Charleston. Who is the government trying to help by passing such a law? Who are the people likely to get apartments under the rent control system?

Brief Solutions to Problem Set G

66. If you think about it, no alternative will work as well.
67. Refer to your lecture notes; often the unintended consequences end up harming the people the policies are designed to help.
68. Medical care is a tough issue – very complicated. Shortages would result.
69. A surplus of corn will result.

70. The article fails to consider credit ratings. Typically a person's credit score is what determines mortgage rates. Credit scores have nothing to do with race, sex, religion, etc.

71. You should see a shortage in the rent-controlled housing market. The government is trying to help poor people or college students, but the relatively well-off are still more likely to end up with the apartments.

Lecture H: Elasticity

72. Has the U.S. government's "war on drugs" been effective? Are there better alternative policies? How does elasticity inform your view on this?

73. Consider the figure below, which illustrates a demand curve for sandwiches. Calculate the $\varepsilon_d = \dfrac{\%\Delta Qd}{\%\Delta P}$ three ways, as listed in *a*, *b*, and *c*. Note that each of these refers to a way to calculate "percentage change," which you must do for both Qd and P.

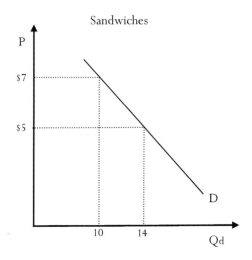

a. Use the "(new-old)/old" as the formula for percentage change, when P falls from $7 to $5. (In this case, $5 is the "new" price, and $7 is the "old" price. Remember that you must calculate percentage change for both P and Qd, then put the numbers into the equation above to get the ε_d.)

b. Use the same formula and calculate ε_d again when P rises from $5 to $7.

c. Use the midpoint method (change/average as the formula for percentage change).

d. Briefly explain why the midpoint method you used in c is superior to the "(new-old)/old" method for calc-ulating percentage change used in the elasticity of demand formula.

Brief Solutions to Problem Set H

72. It would be difficult to argue that the drug was has been successful. We have one of the highest drug use rates of any country. Demand is inelastic, so higher prices (the result of the "war") don't cause use to fall that much. What about education and treatment, instead of enforcement?

73. Recall that the formula for elasticity of demand is the % change in Qd divided by the % change in price.
   a. 1.38 (calculated as 0.4/0.286)
   b. 0.73 (calculated as 0.286/0.4)
   c. 1.0 (calculated as 0.333/0.333)
   d. Using the midpoint method is superior because the direction of the price change doesn't matter. If you use the other method, then you get a different ε_d depending on the direction of price change.

162

Lecture I: Excise Taxes and Deadweight Losses

74. Airlines typically offer discounted round trip fares for reservations made a month in advance, provided the trip includes a Saturday night stay. Since most business travelers make arrangements only a short time before travel, and since firms are reluctant to pay for weekend hotel and food expenses, the discount airline fares are received primarily by vacationers. Why does a policy like this make sense? What does it assume about the relative elasticity of demand for business and vacation travelers? (*H*)

75. If the government imposes an additional tax of $1.00 per pack of cigarettes, due from the sellers, what do you expect to happen to the price of cigarettes? Will it rise by $1.00, more, or less? Why?

76. Does a tax on beer make people better off?

The graph below illustrates the market for Saurman Potted Meat (with 2% real meat), as described on *Space Ghost Coast to Coast*. Use the graph to answer questions 77-84.

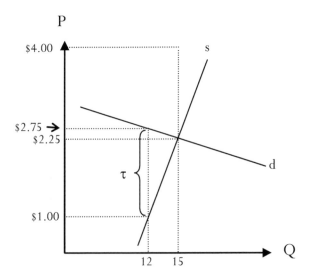

77. According to the graph, what is the initial market price for meat, before the excise tax is imposed?
78. Who is legally responsible for paying the tax to the government?
79. What is the value of the excise tax, τ, per unit of meat?
80. How much of the tax per unit is borne by the producers?
81. How much of the tax per unit is borne by the consumers?
82. How much tax revenue does the government collect on its potted meat excise tax?
83. What is the amount of the deadweight loss caused by the tax? What does the DWL represent?
84. What is the general rule for determining who (buyers or sellers) bears a larger burden of an excise tax?

Brief Solutions to Problem Set I

74. Airlines charge business passengers more because their demand is more inelastic. Vacation travelers generally plan more in advance, and are more sensitive to prices; their demand is more elastic. They get lower prices.
75. The price of cigarettes will probably go up by less than $1, because the demand for cigarettes is not perfectly inelastic.
76. No. How could it? (Maybe people who don't want other people to drink are better off when beer is taxed?)
77. $2.25
78. You can't tell from the graph, but usually excise taxes are imposed on sellers.
79. $1.75
80. $1.25
81. $0.50
82. $1.75 x 12 = $21.00
83. 3 x 1.75 x 0.5 = $2.63; DWL represents lost CS and PS as a result of fewer transactions now taking place.
84. Whoever has the steeper curve bears a larger share of the tax burden, no matter who physically sends the money to the government.

164

Lecture J: International Trade Policy

Consider the figure below in answering questions 85-89.

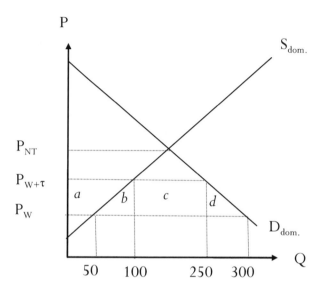

85. What effect does the tariff have on Q of imported goods?
86. As a result of the tariff, what happens to the quantity of domestic production?
87. What happens to domestic consumption as a result of the tariff?
88. What area represents the deadweight loss from the tariff?
89. What is the overall (net) effect of the tariff on society?
90. If instead of a tariff, government imposed an import quota, what quantity would the quota need to be to have the same impact on the market as the tariff shown above?
91. If the quota from question 90 was imposed, what are the different possibilities for area *c* in that case?

Brief Solutions to Problem Set J

85. The quantity of imports falls by 100 (from 250 to 150).
86. Domestic production rises by 50 (from 50 to 100).

87. Domestic consumption falls by 50 (from 300 to 250).
88. Areas b+d
89. Net loss of b+d. (Producers gain a, government gains c, while consumers lose a+b+c+d.)
90. If there was a quota of 150 units, you would get the same overall impact from the tariff shown in the figure. In effect, the quota just restricts the horizontal distance between the S and D curve to a particular quantity.
91. Area c would not be government tariff revenue, but it could represent government revenue if they sell the import permits for their market value. Alternatively, if the foreign country restricts their exports, they can get a higher price for their exports, and get area c. A third possibility is that c would represent a waste of resources because of importers lobbying for the 150 permits.

Lecture K: Market Failures

92. In July 2007, the City of Charleston banned smoking in all public places (with a few exceptions). What might be an economic argument for supporting such a ban? Why can't restaurant/bar/business owners make their own smoking policies for their properties? Should government mandate whether or not you can smoke in your own home? Is there any difference?

93. Why do people sometimes disturb others by talking during movies? Do the talkers and those whom they disturb agree about the rights one acquires when purchasing a movie ticket? How could the owners of movie theaters resolve this conflict? Why don't they do so? (*H*)

94. A large mulberry tree in your neighbor's yard provides you with welcome shade but gives her only a lot of inedible and messy mulberries. She wants to cut the tree down. (*H*)

   a. Does she have the legal right to do so?

   b. You say to her: "I know you hate those messy mulberries, but not nearly as much as I would hate losing the shade." Can you prove your statement? If you can't prove that you value continued shade more than she values a clean yard, can you induce *her* to place a higher value on *her* benefits from leaving the tree than on *her* benefits from cutting it down? (Hint: How do you induce the plumber to decide he would rather clear your drain on a Sunday afternoon than watch his favorite football team?)

95. Buffalo have dwindled in numbers over the years, but cows have increased substantially in their numbers. What explains this? What do you think would happen to the relative size of cattle and buffalo herds if Americans lost their taste for beef and acquired an intense love of buffalo meat? (*H*)

96. Describe the two characteristics required for a good to be considered a pure public good.

97. Suppose Charleston business enterprises are culprits in the pollution of the Ashley River, and the pollution affects fishermen and people who use the river for recreation. How do economists describe this type of pollution? What is its root

cause? (That is, what are the institutional conditions that help create a conflict among people as to how the river can be used?)

For questions 98-102, consider the figure below, which illustrates a situation in which the production of some good creates a negative externality. Perhaps the factory emits smoke that imposes costs on residents near the factory.

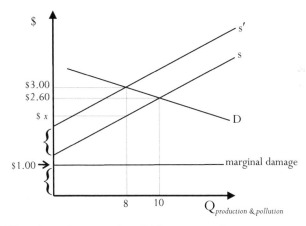

98. What does the quantity of 10 represent?
99. Solve for the value of "$x" in the figure.
100. If the government imposes a Pigouvian tax, what is the appropriate value of the tax per unit of production?
101. What does the curve named s' represent?
102. What is the socially efficient quantity of production and pollution in this case?

Brief Solutions to Problem Set K

92. You could argue that the smoke is a negative externality. But you could also argue that people who are bothered by smoke are not forced to go to restaurants, etc.
93. People talk because the "no talking" rule isn't enforced except in extreme cases. It's generally understood that everyone will be quiet. It's the movie theater's responsibility to enforce the rule, however, they don't want to offend too many people.

94. (a) She has the right to cut the tree down because it's on her property. (b) You can offer to clean up the berries from her yard, or offer to pay her to keep the tree up.
95. Cows are profitable to raise because people like to eat them, much more so than buffalo. Even if people started liking buffalo more, the profit incentive would be there, and ranchers would have the incentive to raise them.
96. Non-excludable: it would be very costly to exclude potential consumers; Non-rival in consumption: one person's consumption of the good does not reduce others' ability to consume.
97. This is an externality, the root cause of which is undefined property rights of the river.
98. This is the quantity that will be produced in the absence of any corrective intervention.
99. $2.00
100. $1.00 per unit of production
101.   s' is the social cost curve, which represents the private cost plus the marginal damage.
102.   Socially efficient level of production is 8.

Lecture L: The U.S. Tax System & Alternatives

103. Even though the Laffer curve shows that lower marginal tax rates (MTRs) can raise as much revenue as higher MTRs, why do you think it is politically popular to "raise taxes on the rich" in America?

104. Explain the advantages and disadvantage of these tax regimes: (a) national sales tax; (b) flat-rate income tax; (c) the current income tax system (progressive rate income tax); (d) head tax

105. In what sense is the current U.S. tax code wasteful of resources? How does the "fair tax" overcome this waste?

Brief Solutions to Problem Set L

103. Probably envy or "fairness." Some people just like the idea of "sticking it to the rich." Others may think it is fair if the "rich" pay more.

104. (a) The national sales tax is good because it doesn't penalize productivity or work, and it's easy to implement. No real disadvantages. (b) The flat-rate income tax is slightly better than what we currently have. If you eliminate all the complications, it would be a vast improvement. (c) This is what we have; it's probably the worst of all options, except (d). (d) A head tax is just a flat tax per person. At the 2015 government spending level, it would be about $12,200 per person. The advantage would be you don't need IRS and tax accountants, etc. Disadvantage: Bill Gates gets a really low tax, while some poor people can't afford the tax at all.

105. There's a huge amount of resources wasted in an effort to comply with the tax code. People was billions of hours of time (and billions of $) each year filing tax forms. All tax compliance activities are a complete social waste. A fair tax would eliminate most of this waste, since collection of the tax would be as simple as collecting state sales taxes.

EXAMPLE TEST QUESTIONS

The test questions presented here are good examples of how I write multiple choice questions. But you should not expect to see these specific questions on exams. The exams may also include short answer questions and graphical problems.

Your best strategy for preparing for exams is to make sure you *understand the concepts*, rather than memorizing stuff. I urge you not to attempt to memorize these test questions, but rather, try to understand why the correct answers are what they are.

If you have questions about any of these, feel free to come talk to me during office hours, or ask me in class.

Note that some of these questions may not be directly related to material we cover in class this semester.

Example Test Questions over Lectures A – E
[answers are on p. 176]

1. If the price is not currently at the equilibrium price, what can you say about the number of transactions that will occur in the market, relative to the number of transactions that would occur at P_e?
   a. The number of transactions will be higher than at P_e as long as the price is <u>lower</u> than the equilibrium level.
   b. The number of transactions will be higher than at P_e as long as the price is <u>higher</u> than the equilibrium level.
   c. The number of transactions is maximized at the P_e, so any other price will result in fewer transactions.
   d. Since the economy is based on greed, less greed means higher well-being. This implies that the lower the price, the <u>more</u> transactions will occur.

2. If quantity demanded equals quantity supplied, then
   a. prices signal less scarcity in the market.
   b. there may be a shortage in the money market.
   c. demand is downward sloping.
   d. there cannot be a shortage or a surplus.
   e. supply is greater than quantity demanded.

3. Suppose plague-killed cows are a major input in the production of Erby's restaurant's sandwiches. Further, assume that Erby's sandwiches and stomach pumps are complementary goods. What would you expect to happen *in the market for stomach pumps* if the supply of plague-killed cows decreases?
   a. P increases, Q falls
   b. P increases, Q increases
   c. P falls, Q falls
   d. P falls, Q increases

4. If supply decreases and demand decreases, the following will happen:
   a. equilibrium quantity rises
   b. P rises
   c. P falls
   d. equilibrium quantity falls
   e. [none of the above]

5. John's income increases and as a result his demand for Widespread concert tickets increases. Which of the following follows from this statement?
   a. Widespread concert tickets are inferior goods for John.
   b. Widespread concert tickets are normal goods for everyone in the economy.
   c. Widespread concert tickets are inferior goods for everyone in the economy.
   d. Widespread concert tickets are normal goods for John.
   e. Widespread concert tickets are good for economists.

Please refer to the following figure for questions 6 & 7. Two countries, Colombia and South Africa, are producing diamonds and emeralds.

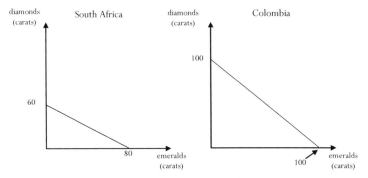

6. If South Africa and Colombia each specialize in the good that they have the comparative advantage in, South Africa will produce _____ and Colombia will produce _____ .
   a. diamonds, diamonds
   b. diamonds, emeralds
   c. emeralds, diamonds
   d. emeralds, emeralds
   e. [none of the above]

7. Which of the following ratios is a suitable terms of trade?
   a. 3d : 1e
   b. 3d : 5e
   c. 3d : 2e
   d. 3d : 3.5e

8. Marginal utility (or marginal benefit)
   a. is constant so long as price is constant.
   b. can be fixed in the short-run.
   c. is total utility divided by the number of units consumed.
   d. declines as quantity consumed increases over a given period of time.

9. Suppose tacos and burritos are substitute goods. If the supply of tacos decreases, what happens in the market for burritos?
   a. P increases, Q falls
   b. P increases, Q increases
   c. P falls, Q falls
   d. P falls, Q increases

174

10. Which of the following *does* *not* increase or decrease (shift) demand?
    a. a decrease in the price of a substitute good
    b. a change in income
    c. a surplus
    d. [all of the above shift demand]

11. If the consumers and producers of computers suddenly expect the market price to fall drastically next month, which of the following can you say should most likely happen this month?
    a. price falls
    b. quantity falls
    c. price rises
    d. quantity rises

12. What kinds of factors determine comparative advantage?
    a. differences in technology and resource endowments
    b. legislation arising mainly from the European Economic Community (EEC)
    c. different consumption preferences
    d. [none of the above]

13. In *the market for cameras*, an increase in the price of film would cause a
    a. decrease in quantity supplied.
    b. decrease in price.
    c. decrease in demand.
    d. [all of the above]

14. Exchange arises in a free market as a result of
    a. government planning.
    b. individuals' inherent self-interest.
    c. the warm friendly feeling it generates.
    d. random behavior.

15. Ester, a rational human being, will eat carrots until
    a. the total benefit is equated to the total cost.

b. the marginal benefit of the last carrot equals the marginal cost of the last carrot.

c. the marginal benefit of the last carrot is infinite.

d. the full cost is minimized.

e. [none of the above]

16. As a good becomes more plentiful (or less scarce) in the market

a. government should enact a law to prevent the price from rising.

b. the price of that good should increase to reflect the decreased scarcity.

c. the price of that good should decrease to reflect the decreased scarcity.

d. a shortage of the good will result.

17. The *ceteris paribus* assumption is that we assume...

a. everything else changes in the same direction.

b. everything else changes in the opposite direction.

c. everything else remains constant.

d. everything else changes in completely unpredictable ways.

18. An increase in supply is shown as a _____ the supply curve. After something changes to increase supply, then for sellers to still be willing to produce and sell a particular quantity, they _____.

a. leftward shift of ; insist on higher prices from consumers.

b. rightward shift of ; are willing to accept lower prices from consumers.

c. movement rightward along ; must see an increase in demand.

d. movement leftward along ; must see a decrease in demand.

19. The law of decreasing marginal utility means that

a. as consumption increases, the total benefit from consuming falls.

b. as consumption increases, the additional benefit from consuming one more unit is less than the benefit from the previous unit.

c. as consumption increases, the consumer gets the same amount of benefit as she did from each previous unit of consumption.

d. as consumption increases, the total benefit the consumer gets from consuming additional units increases at an increasing rate.

Answers to Example Test Questions over Lectures A – E

1c, 2d, 3c, 4d, 5d, 6c, 7d, 8d, 9b, 10c, 11a, 12a, 13d, 14b, 15b, 16c, 17c, 18b, 19b

Example Test Questions over Lectures F – J
[answers are on p. 182]

1. A $1.50 excise tax on cigarettes (to be legally paid by suppliers) will
    a. raise the market price of cigarettes by exactly $1.50.
    b. raise the market price of cigarettes by more than $1.50.
    c. raise the market price of cigarettes by less than $1.50.
    d. will decrease the demand for cigarettes.

2. Economic theory predicts that a minimum wage law will result in
    a. a higher standard of living for all Americans.
    b. lower unemployment for low-skilled workers and higher average wages.
    c. higher wages for some low-skilled workers, but unemployment for others.
    d. full employment and reduced poverty.

3. The condition for productive efficiency in a particular industry, i.e., producing a given quantity of output at the minimum total cost, is $MC_A = MC_B = \cdots = MC_N$, where N is the number of firms producing. (This means the marginal cost of production for all firms must equal.) If this condition is <u>not</u> met, the total cost of producing a given quantity in the market *could be decreased* because
    a. the total cost is minimized only where the quantities produced by all firms are equal.
    b. the total cost for all firms must be equal; this occurs where the marginal costs for all firms equal.
    c. the last unit from one firm (with higher *MC*) could be given up in exchange for an additional unit of output from another firm (with lower *MC*).
    d. the last unit from the firm with the lowest *MC* could be given up in exchange for an additional unit from the firm with the highest *MC*.

4. Although lawmakers legislated a fifty-fifty division of the payment of the FICA tax,
   a. the employee now is required by law to pay a larger percentage of the tax than the employer.
   b. employers are no longer required by law to pay their portion of the tax.
   c. the same outcome would occur if the entire tax had been levied on only the employee or only on the employer.
   d. the employer now is required by law to pay a larger percentage of the tax.

5. Suppose a market was originally at its equilibrium. If the government imposes an effective price floor or price ceiling, the quantity of mutually-beneficial, voluntary transactions
   a. will rise, since scarcity is the catalyst for these government policies.
   b. will increase as the result of a price ceiling, but will decrease as the result of a price floor.
   c. cannot be predicted.
   d. will remain unchanged, since there can be only one equilibrium quantity.
   e. must decrease as the result of either policy.

6. Price floors tend to ignore the interests of _____; price ceilings act to promote the interests of _____.
   a. producers; producers
   b. consumers; consumers
   c. consumers; producers
   d. producers; consumers

As a part of her (unsuccessful) 2003 campaign for California governor, porn star Mary Carey proposed an excise tax on breast implants, arguing that it would raise millions of dollars of revenue for the state. In support of her proposal, she offered the following graphical analysis in a press conference. (Okay, she didn't really show this graph. But go with it.) Use the information provided in the figure to answer questions 7 – 9.

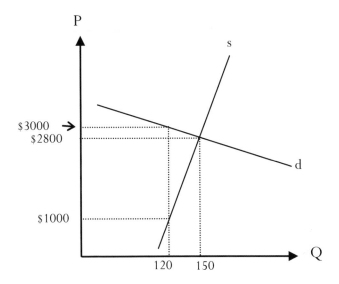

7. According to the figure, on which party has the excise tax been <u>legally placed</u>?
   a. buyers
   b. sellers
   c. both equally
   d. neither
   e. [This cannot be determined from figure.]

8. If the tax was imposed only in California, many potential consumers would probably just go to other states to have the procedure, thereby avoiding the tax. What effect does this issue have on the figure shown above?
   a. This would make the supply curve fairly inelastic, as it is shown.
   b. This would make the demand curve fairly elastic, as it is shown.
   c. This would make the supply curve fairly elastic.
   d. This would make the demand curve fairly inelastic.

9. What is the amount of the excise tax (per procedure) being charged by the government?
   a. $200   b. $1000   c. $1800   d. $2000   e. $3000

The figure below illustrates the domestic market for Chia Pets. Suppose a tariff is imposed on imported Chia Pets. Use the figure to answer questions 10-11.

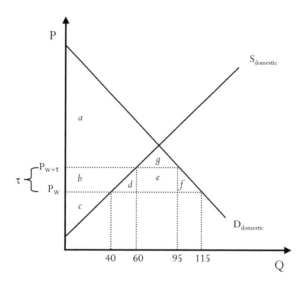

10. <u>By how much does the quantity of imports change</u> as a result of the tariff being imposed?
   a. imports decrease by 40
   b. imports increase by 75
   c. imports decrease by 35
   d. imports decrease by 75

11. What is the effect on domestic producers as a result of the tariff being imposed?
   a. producers gain f.
   b. producers gain b.
   c. producers gain e.
   d. producers gain e+g.
   e. producers gain c.

12. Suppose you're selling moonshine. If you lower price 10% and Q_D rises by 15%, then the elasticity of demand is _____ .
   a. unit elastic

b. $\varepsilon_d > 1$

c. $\varepsilon_d < 1$

d. [none of the above]

13. If demand is more elastic than supply, then who will bear a greater share of the excise tax burden?

   a. It depends on the statutory tax burden (i.e., who is legally required to send the tax money to government).

   b. The consumer will bear a greater portion of the tax burden ONLY if the consumer is legally required to send the tax to the government

   c. The consumer will bear a greater portion of the tax burden regardless of who sends the tax revenue to the government.

   d. The producer will bear a greater share of the tax burden.

   e. The producer and consumer will likely equally share the tax burden, since that is the only fair solution.

14. You work the door at the Rooftop Bar, and your boss has asked you to calculate the elasticity of demand for entrance to the bar. On two otherwise identical Friday nights, you implement different cover charges. On the night when you charge $5, 200 people enter the bar. On the night when you charge $3, 400 people enter the bar. Using these two data points and the midpoint method, calculate the elasticity of demand (ε_d). Based on your answer, and assuming that the ε_d remains the same at all prices, how should the bar adjust its cover charge if its only interest is in increasing total revenue from the cover charge?

   a. It should raise prices, since demand is inelastic.

   b. It should lower prices, since demand is elastic.

   c. It doesn't matter since demand is unit-elastic.

   d. It should no longer charge at the door, since demand is infinitely elastic.

182

15. Why would you be more likely to see racial discrimination occurring in rent-controlled cities, compared to non-rent-controlled cities?
    a. If, as the result of the rent-controls, landlords cannot allocate apartments based on price, they must use some form of non-price rationing.
    b. Statistically, rent-controlled communities simply have more racists.
    c. Rent-control laws are most prevalent where there is a high proportion of whites; these are the people most likely to discriminate against other races.
    d. There is no legitimate reason to expect any difference in racial discrimination between rent-controlled and non-rent-controlled cities.

Answers to Example Test Questions over Lectures F – J

1c, 2c, 3c, 4c, 5e, 6b, 7e, 8b, 9d, 10a, 11b, 12b, 13d, 14b, 15a

Example Test Questions over Lectures K – M
[answers are on p. 186]

1. A negative externality exists when
   a. private costs equal social costs.
   b. social costs exceed private costs.
   c. private costs exceed social costs.
   d. the quantity produced is too low.

2. The South Carolina income tax reaches its highest bracket of 7% at an income of around $14,000. Most people can simply think of this as a...
   a. flat tax of 7%.
   b. trivial tax which is not likely to affect them.
   c. being included in federal income taxes, so they don't have to worry about it.
   d. the same thing as the 7% state sales tax.

3. The idea that clearly defined property rights are sufficient to internalize an externality is called the
   a. Coase theorem.
   b. law of diminishing returns.
   c. internalizationality theorem.
   d. "shame spiral" theory.

4. A progressive tax system is one in which
   a. individuals with a higher income pay a greater dollar amount of taxes.
   b. individuals with a lower income pay more tax dollars.
   c. individuals with a higher income pay a higher average tax rate.
   d. people with a low income pay a higher average tax rate.

5. Public goods are unique in that
   a. all people can consume them jointly.
   b. everyone pays a different price for them.
   c. they are both rival and excludable.
   d. only the poor are allowed to consume them.

6. According to public goods theory, must "health care" be provided by government for it to be provided efficiently?
   a. No, since health care is rival and excludable.
   b. Yes, since health care is non-rival and non-excludable.
   c. Yes, since having a healthy population is consistent with the public good.
   d. No, since having people live too long is inconsistent with the public good.

Suppose the government is considering adopting an income tax based on daily earnings, and there are two proposals for what the tax rate schedule should look like. These are listed in the columns below, (1) and (2). Use the information in the table to answer questions 7-9.

Income	Marginal Tax Rate (schedule 1)	Marginal Tax Rate (schedule 2)
$0 – 10	10%	20%
$11 – 20	30%	20%
$21 – and above	80%	20%

7. Which tax rate schedule is "progressive"?
   a. MTR schedule 1.
   b. MTR schedule 2.
   c. [neither 1 nor 2]
   d. [both 1 and 2]

8. What would be your approximate tax due under each tax schedule, if your income is $30?
   a. Schedule 1: $12; Schedule 2: $6
   b. Schedule 1: $24; Schedule 2: $6
   c. Schedule 1: $80; Schedule 2: $20
   d. Schedule 1: $40; Schedule 2: $12

9. Would you expect any difference between the two tax rate structures, in terms of their effects on a person's incentive to work harder to earn a higher income?

a. Neither tax rate structure should affect the incentive to work, since people need to earn income.

b. The MTRs listed in (1) would tend to discourage work and productivity, as marginal tax rates rise sharply as income rises.

c. The MTRs listed in (2) would discourage work and productivity; since the MTR does not rise with income, the worker is not likely to feel that they are helping society by paying their fair share of taxes.

d. What is Walker talking about? People love taxes! That's the only reason people want to work – to pay taxes!

10. When externalities exist, buyers and sellers
   a. neglect the external effects of their actions but the private market equilibrium is still efficient.
   b. do not neglect the external effects of their actions and the private market equilibrium is efficient.
   c. neglect the external effects of their actions and the private market equilibrium is not efficient.
   d. do not neglect the external effects of their actions and the private market equilibrium is not efficient.

11. Merton Miller, a Nobel laureate in economics has written that if the current tax system was revised (e.g., changed to a flat tax or national sales tax), "armies of tax lawyers and accountants would lose their jobs and be forced to enter productive employment." This sentiment reflects what idea from the lecture on taxes?
   a. Taxes are not fair.
   b. Tax compliance costs are very high.
   c. Taxes should be raised on wealthy people.
   d. Republicans are corrupt.
   e. The current tax system is the "least bad" tax system possible.

Mr. Montgomery Burns' nuclear power plant (in Springfield) pollutes a nearby river. The pot-smoking, womanizing, and tax-cheating Mayor Quimby wishes to decrease the amount of pollution into the river. Given this information, along with the information in the graph below, answer questions 12 & 13.

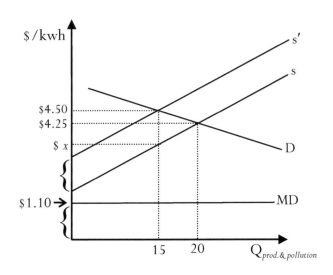

12. What should the value of "$ x" be in the figure above?
    a. $4.00   b. $3.75   c. $3.40   d. $3.15
    e. [This can't be determined.]

13. What is the socially efficient level of production/pollution?
    a. 0   b. more than 0, but less than 15   c. >20
    d. 15   e. more than 15, but less than 20

14. The tax principle of "vertical equity" says that
    a. all people should pay the same dollar amount in taxes.
    b. individuals with lower income should not pay any taxes.
    c. individuals with higher income should pay more in taxes.
    d. people who live in democracies should not have to pay taxes.

Answers to Example Test Questions over Lectures K – M

1b, 2a, 3a, 4c, 5a, 6a, 7a, 8a, 9b, 10c, 11b, 12c, 13d, 14c

Notes

Made in the USA
Columbia, SC
10 January 2020